P-PZ
TABLES

LANGUAGE AND LITERATURE TABLES

Library of Congress Classification

1998 EDITION

Prepared by the
Cataloging Policy
and Support Office,
Library Services

Library of Congress, Cataloging Distribution Service, Washington, D.C.

The additions and changes in Class P-PZ adopted while this work was in press will be cumulated and printed in List 272 of *LC Classification— Additions and Changes*

Library of Congress Cataloging-in-Publication Data

Library of Congress.
    Library of Congress classification. P–PZ tables, Language and Literature tables / prepared by the Cataloging Policy and Support Office, Library Services. — 1998 ed.
        p. cm.
    ISBN 0–8444–0966–9

    1. Classification, Library of Congress. 2. Classification—Books—Philology. 3. Classification—Books—Linguistics. 4. Classification—Books—Literatures. I. — Library of Congress. Cataloging Policy and Support Office. II. Title.
Z696.U5P88 1998
025.4'33—dc21   98–39699
                                                      CIP

For sale by the Cataloging Distribution Service, Library of Congress, Washington, DC 20541

PREFACE

The first edition of the standardized tables used in Class P, developed by Milicent Wewerka, now a senior cataloging policy specialist, was published in 1982. This 1998 edition cumulates all changes that have been made to the tables since that date. The 1982 edition included a conversion table showing the old table numbers that had been used in the P schedules prior to the development of these standardized tables, and the corresponding new table numbers. Since these standardized tables have now been in use for sixteen years, the conversion table is not included in this 1998 edition. Those who continue to find this conversion information useful may wish to retain the earlier edition.

This edition has been produced using a new automated system developed at the Library of Congress for this purpose. The system will allow for the production of new editions on a regular and frequent basis.

In 1992, Rebecca Guenther, Network Development and MARC Standards Office, began overseeing the conversion of Library of Congress Classification data to machine-readable form using the provisionally approved USMARC format for classification data. In 1993-1994, the Cataloging Distribution Service developed programs for producing printed classification schedules from the MARC records in cooperation with Lawrence Buzard, editor of classification schedules, Paul Weiss, senior cataloging policy specialist, and Rebecca Guenther. The Cataloging Distribution Service also coordinated the layout and design of the new schedules.

Milicent Wewerka proofread and edited the data for the P tables after their conversion to the MARC classification format.

New or revised numbers and captions are added to the L.C. Classification schedules and tables as a result of development proposals made by the cataloging staff of the Library of Congress and cooperating institutions. Upon approval of these proposals by the weekly editorial meeting of the Cataloging Policy and Support Office, new classification records are created or existing records are revised in the master classification database. The Classification Editorial Team, consisting of Lawrence Buzard, editor, and Barry Bellinger, Kent Griffiths, Nancy Jones, and Dorothy Thomas, assistant editors, is responsible for creating new classification records, maintaining the master database, and creating index terms for the captions.

Thompson A. Yee, Acting Chief
Cataloging Policy and Support Office

June 1998

	Periodicals. Serials
1.A1-A3	International
1.A4-Z	English and American
2	French
3	German
9	Other (not A-Z)
10	Annuals. Yearbooks, etc.
	Societies
11.A1-A3	International
11.A4-Z	English and American
12	French
13	German
19	Other (not A-Z)
21	Congresses
	Collections (nonserial)
23	Texts, sources, etc.
	Class here only collections of texts
	For readers, see 117
	For texts and studies, see 25
25	Monographs. Studies
26.A-Z	Studies in honor of a particular person or institution, A-Z
27	Individual authors
31	Encyclopedias
33	Atlases, maps, charts, tables, etc.
	Cf. 777, Linguistic geography
	Philosophy. Theory. Method
35	General works
37	Relations
	History of philology
	Cf. 65-69.5, Study and teaching
	Cf. P-PZ1 75-87, History of the language
51	General works
52	General special
	By period
53	Earliest
54	Middle Ages
55	Renaissance
	Modern
57	General works
58	19th-20th centuries
60.A-Z	By region or country, A-Z
	Biography, memoirs, etc.
63	Collective
64.A-Z	Individual, A-Z
	Study and teaching. Research
65	General works
66	General special
	By period
	see P-PZ1 53-58, 75-87, etc.
68.A-Z	By region or country, A-Z
69.A-Z	By school, A-Z
69.5.A-Z	By research institute, A-Z

	General works
70	Early to 1800
71	Treatises (Philology, General)
	General special
73	General works
74	Relation to other languages
74.5	Language data processing
74.7	Language standardization and variation
74.73	Political aspects
	Cf. 479.P6, Rhetoric
	Cf. 830.P6, Slang
74.75	Social aspects
74.8	Spoken language
74.85	Language acquisition
	History of the language
75	General works
	Early, see 53
77	Middle Ages
79	(15th)-16th century
81	(16th)-17th century
83	(17th)-18th century
85	19th century
87	20th century
	By region, see 700-840
93	Outlines
95	Popular
97	Script
	Grammar
99	Comparative (Two or more languages)
101	Historical
	General works
103	To 1800
105	1800-
107	General special
	Textbooks
108	History and criticism
109	Early to 1870
111	1870-1949
112	1950-
112.5	Self-instructors
112.7	Audiovisual instructors
	Readers
112.9	History and criticism
113	Series
115	Primers. Primary grade readers
117	Intermediate and advanced
118	Outlines, syllabi, tables, etc.
119	Examination questions, etc.
120.A-Z	Manuals for special classes of students, A-Z
120.C6	Commercial
	Cf. HF5719, Business report writing; HF5721, Business correspondence
120.F37	Farmers

	Grammar
	Manuals for special
	classes of students, A-Z -- Continued
120.F58	Fishermen
120.G35	Gardeners
120.L52	Library employees
120.M3	Medical personnel
120.M87	Musicians. Musicologists
120.P45	Personnel department employees
120.P47	Petroleum workers
120.P64	Police
120.P76	Professionals (General)
120.R4	Restaurant personnel
120.S34	School employees
	Self-instructors, see 112.5
120.S45	Servants
120.S57	Social workers
120.S58	Soldiers
120.T42	Technical
121	Conversation. Phrase books
123	Plays for acting in schools and colleges
	Idioms, errors, etc., see 460
127.A-Z	Readers on special subjects, A-Z
127.A45	Africa
127.A46	Africa, North
127.A7	Art
127.B5	Biography
127.C5	Civilization
127.C6	Commerce
127.C8	Current events
127.D48	Detective and mystery stories
127.D7	Drama
127.E25	Economics
127.E38	Education
127.E83	Ethnology
127.F35	Fantastic fiction
127.F54	Finance
127.F66	Folk literature
127.F7	France
127.G4	Geography
127.G44	Geology
127.H48	Hispanic Americans
127.H5	History
127.I85	Italy
127.J35	Japan
127.J68	Journalism
127.L34	Latin America
127.L37	Law
127.L4	Legends
127.L45	Lermontov, Mikhail IU r′evich, 1814-1841
	Literature
	see P-PZ1 113-117
127.M3	Mathematics

	Grammar
	Readers on special
	subjects, A-Z -- Continued
127.M38	Medicine
127.M39	Mexican-Americans
127.M4	Mexico
127.M48	Military art and science
127.M5	Minorities
127.M87	Music
	Mystery stories, see 127.D48
127.N26	Names
127.N27	National characteristics
127.N3	Naval science
127.N48	New Mexico
127.N49	Newspapers
127.O33	Occupations
127.P45	Philosophy
127.P48	Physics
127.P63	Poetry
127.P64	Poland
127.P66	Political science
127.P8	Public administration
127.P87	Pushkin, Aleksandr Sergeevich, 1799-1837
127.R34	Railroads
127.R86	Russian history
127.S4	Science
127.S6	Social sciences
	Soviet history, see 127.R86
127.S63	Spain
127.T47	Theater
127.T49	Theology
127.T68	Tourist trade
	Travels, see 127.V68
127.V68	Voyages and travels
127.W37	War
	Textbooks for foreign speakers
127.8	Theory, methods, etc., for teachers
128	General
129.A-Z	By language, A-Z
	Phonology
	Including phonemics
	Cf. 153-165, Alphabet
131	General works
	Phonetics
135	General works
136	Palatalization
137	Pronunciation
139	Accent
139.3	Clitics
139.5	Intonation
139.7	Prosodic analysis
140	Phonetics of the sentence (Sandhi)
	Orthography. Spelling

	Grammar
	Parts of speech (Morphology
	and Syntax)
	Verb -- Continued
271	General works
276	Person
280	Number
285	Voice
290	Mood
301	Tense
306	Aspects of verbal action
	Infinitive and participle
311	General works
312	Participle, gerund, etc.
315.A-Z	Special classes of verbs, A-Z
315.A8	Auxiliary
315.F3	Factitive
315.I46	Imperative
315.I6	Impersonal
	Intransitive/Transitive, see 315.T72
315.I8	Irregular
315.P4	Periphrastic
315.P52	Phrasal
315.R4	Reflexive
315.T72	Transitive/Intransitive
317.A-Z	Particular verbs, A-Z
318	Other. Miscellaneous
	Particle
321	General works
325	Adverb
335	Preposition
340	Postposition
345	Conjunction
355	Interjection
359.A-Z	Other special, A-Z
359.C54	Clitics
359.N4	Negatives
	Syntax
	General
361	General works
365	Outlines
369	General special
	Sentences
375	General arrangement, etc.
380	Order of words
385	Order of clauses
390	Clauses
395	Other special
398.A-Z	Other aspects, A-Z
398.A35	Agreement
398.A52	Anaphora
398.A66	Apposition
398.C38	Causative

	Grammar
	Other aspects, A-Z -- Continued
398.C65	Complement
398.D42	Definiteness
398.D44	Deixis
398.D46	Dependency grammar
398.D47	Determiners
398.E95	Existential constructions
398.G73	Grammatical categories
398.H65	Honorific
398.I57	Interrogative
398.L62	Locative constructions
398.M63	Modality
398.T46	Temporal constructions
(400.A-Z)	Grammatical usage of particular authors, A-Z
	see the author in classes PA-PT
	Style. Composition. Rhetoric
	For study and teaching, see 65-69.5
410	General works
420	Textbooks
430	Outlines, questions, exercises and specimens. List of
	subjects
(433.A-Z)	Special authors, A-Z
	see the author in classes PA-PT
434	Discourse analysis
	Special parts of rhetoric
435	Style. Invention, narration, etc.
440	Other special. Figures, tropes, allegory, etc.
445	Choice of words. Vocabulary, etc.
450	Punctuation
460	Idioms. Errors. Blunders
	Special classes of composition
471	Essays
473	Lectures
474	Newspaper style
475	Scientific papers
477	Precis writing
478	Report writing
479.A-Z	Other, A-Z
479.P6	Political literature
	Letter writing
481	Early to 1800
	1800-
483	General works
	Business
	see HF5721+
	Etiquette
	see BJ2100+
	Love letters
	see HQ801.3+
485	Textbooks
	Specimens. Collections
495	Early to 1850/1870

	Style. Composition.
	Rhetoric
	Special classes
	of composition
	Letter writing
	Specimens. Collections -- Continued
497	1850/1870-
	Translating
	For special subjects, see classes B-Z, e.g. T11.5,
	Technology
498	General works
499	Machine translating
	Including research
	Prosody. Metrics. Rhytmics
501	History of the science
	General works
504	Early to 1800
505	1800-
509	Textbooks
511	Versification (Gradus ad Parnassum)
	Rhyme
517	General works
519	Rhyming dictionaries
521.A-Z	Special. By form, A-Z
521.E6	Epic
521.L9	Lyric
531.A-Z	Special meters, A-Z
531.A3	Alexandrine
531.D4	Decasyllable
531.F8	Free verse
541	Other special
	Including epithets
(551)	Special authors
	see the author in classes PA-PT
559	Rhythm
561	Rhythm in prose
567	Lexicology
	Etymology
571	Treatises
574	Popular works
576	Names (General)
	For personal names see CS2300+, for place names, see
	G104+, (General) or classes D - F for names of
	specific continents or countries
580	Dictionaries (exclusively etymological)
582.A-Z	Special elements. By language, A-Z
582.A3	Foreign elements (General)
	Cf. 670, Dictionaries
583	Other special
584	Folk etymology
585	Semantics
591	Synonyms. Antonyms
593	Paronyms

	Etymology -- Continued
595	Homonyms
596	Eponyms
597	Onomatopoeic words
599.A-Z	Particular words, A-Z
	Lexicography
601	Periodicals. Societies. Serials. Collections (nonserial)
611	General works
	Biography of lexicographers, see 63-64
617	Criticism, etc., of particular dictionaries
	Dictionaries
	Dictionaries with definitions in same language
620	Early to 1800
	1800-
625	General
628	Minor, abridged, school dictionaries
629	Picture dictionaries
630	Supplementary dictionaries. Dictionaries of new words
635	Dictionaries with definitions in two or more languages, or dictionaries of two or more languages with definitions in one language
640	Dictionaries with definitions in English
645.A-Z	Dictionaries with definitions in other languages. By language, A-Z
	Dictionaries exclusively etymological, see 580
650	Dictionaries of particular periods (other than periods separately specified elsewhere)
(655)	Dictionaries of particular authors see the author in classes PA-PT
660	Dictionaries of names
	Cf. 673, Foreign words
	Cf. CS2300+, Personal and family names
	Dictionaries, etc. of obsolete, archaic words and provincialisms
667	General
	Local provincialisms, see 701-780
	Dictionaries of foreign words
670	General
673	Names
	Special. By language, see 582.A-Z
	Other special lists
680	Glossaries
(683.A-Z)	By subject, A-Z see the subject in classes A-N, Q-Z
689	Dictionaries of terms and phrases
691	Word frequency lists
	For research on word frequency, etc., in connection with machine translating, see 499
692	Reverse indexes
693	Abbreviations, Lists of

	Linguistic geography. Dialects, etc.
	For nearly all of the more important languages spoken in Europe special schemes for dialects have been made
700	Linguistic geography
	Cf. 777, Atlases
	Dialects, provincialisms, etc.
	For language standardization and variation, see 74.7
701	Periodicals. Collections
707	Collections of texts, etc.
710	General works
	Grammar
720	General works
725	Phonology. Phonetics
735	Morphology
750	Syntax
760	Other
770	Dictionaries
777	Atlases, maps, charts, tables
780.A-Z	Local. By region, place, etc., A-Z
	Slang. Argot
800	Collections
810	General works
815	Dictionaries. Lists
820	Texts
830.A-Z	Special topics, A-Z
830.B88	Butchers' language
830.C35	Cant
830.C6	Court and courtiers language
830.C84	Cultural property
830.N63	Nobility
830.O27	Obscene words
830.O65	Opera production
830.P6	Political language
830.P74	Prisoners' language
830.R3	Railroad language
830.S64	Soldiers' language
830.S66	Sports language
830.S82	Students' language
830.W65	Women's language
830.W67	World War II
830.Y68	Youth
840.A-Z	Special local, A-Z

	Periodicals. Serials
1	International. English and American. French. German
3	Other (not A-Z)
4	Annuals. Yearbooks, etc.
	Societies
5	International. English and American. French. German
7	Other (not A-Z)
9	Congresses
	Collections (nonserial)
11	Texts, sources, etc.
	Class here only collections of texts
	For readers, see 71
	For texts and studies, see 13
13	Monographs. Studies
14.A-Z	Studies in honor of a particular person or institution, A-Z
15	Individual authors
19	Encyclopedias
20	Atlases, maps, charts, tables
	Cf. 393, Linguistic geography
	Philosophy. Theory. Method
21	General works
23	Relations
	History of philology
	Cf. 35-39.5, Study and teaching
	Cf. P-PZ2 45-51, History of the language
25	General works
26	General special
	By period
27	Earliest. Middle Ages. Renaissance
29	Modern
31.A-Z	By region or country, A-Z
	Biography, memoirs, etc.
33	Collective
34.A-Z	Individual, A-Z
	Study and teaching. Research
35	General works
36	General special
	By period
	see P-PZ2 27-29, 45-51, etc.
38.A-Z	By region or country, A-Z
39.A-Z	By school, A-Z
39.5.A-Z	By research institute, A-Z
	General works
40	Early to 1800
41	Treatises (Philology, General)
	General special
43	General works
44	Relation to other languages
44.5	Language data processing
44.7	Language standardization and variation
44.73	Political aspects
	Cf. 421.P6, Slang

	General works
	General special -- Continued
44.75	Social aspects
44.8	Spoken language
44.85	Language acquisition
	History of the language
45	General works
	Early, see 27
47	Middle Ages. (15th)-16th century
49	(16th)-18th century
51	19th-20th century
	By region, see 350-431
55	Outlines
57	Popular
58	Script
	Grammar
59	Comparative (Two or more languages)
61	Historical
	General works
63	To 1800
64	1800-
65	General special
	Textbooks
65.5	History and criticism
66	Early to 1870
67	1870-1949
67.3	1950-
67.5	Self-instructors
67.7	Audiovisual instructors
	Readers
67.9	History and criticism
68	Series
69	Primers. Primary grade readers
71	Intermediate and advanced
71.3	Outlines, syllabi, tables, etc.
71.5	Examination questions, etc.
72.A-Z	Manuals for special classes of students, A-Z
72.C6	Commercial
	Cf. HF5719, Business report writing; HF5721, Business correspondence
72.F37	Farmers
72.F58	Fishermen
72.G35	Gardeners
72.L52	Library employees
72.M3	Medical personnel
72.M87	Musicians. Musicologists
72.P45	Personnel department employees
72.P47	Petroleum workers
72.P64	Police
72.P76	Professionals (General)
72.R4	Restaurant personnel
72.S34	School employees
	Self-instructors, see 67.5

	Grammar
	Manuals for special
	classes of students, A-Z -- Continued
72.S45	Servants
72.S57	Social workers
72.S58	Soldiers
72.T42	Technical
73	Conversation. Phrase books
74	Plays for acting in schools and colleges
	Idioms, errors, etc., see 260
74.2.A-Z	Readers on special subjects, A-Z
74.2.A45	Africa
74.2.A46	Africa, North
74.2.A7	Art
74.2.B5	Biography
74.2.C5	Civilization
74.2.C6	Commerce
74.2.C8	Current events
74.2.D48	Detective and mystery stories
74.2.D7	Drama
74.2.E25	Economics
74.2.E38	Education
74.2.E83	Ethnology
74.2.F35	Fantastic fiction
74.2.F54	Finance
74.2.F66	Folk literature
74.2.F7	France
74.2.G4	Geography
74.2.G44	Geology
74.2.H48	Hispanic Americans
74.2.H5	History
74.2.I8	Israel
74.2.I85	Italy
74.2.J35	Japan
74.2.J68	Journalism
74.2.L34	Latin America
74.2.L37	Law
74.2.L4	Legends
74.2.L45	Lermontov, Mikhail IU r′evich, 1814-1841
	Literature
	see P-PZ2 68-71
74.2.M3	Mathematics
74.2.M38	Medicine
74.2.M39	Mexican-American
74.2.M4	Mexico
74.2.M48	Military art and science
74.2.M5	Minorities
74.2.M87	Music
	Mystery stories, see 74.2.D48
74.2.N26	Names
74.2.N27	National characteristics
74.2.N3	Naval science
74.2.N48	New Mexico

	Grammar
	Readers on special
	subjects, A-Z -- Continued
74.2.N49	Newspapers
74.2.O33	Occupations
74.2.P45	Philosophy
74.2.P48	Physics
74.2.P63	Poetry
74.2.P64	Poland
74.2.P66	Political science
74.2.P8	Public administration
74.2.P87	Pushkin, Aleksandr Sergeevich, 1799-1837
74.2.R34	Railroads
74.2.R86	Russian history
74.2.S4	Science
74.2.S6	Social sciences
	Soviet history, see 74.2.R86
74.2.S63	Spain
74.2.T47	Theater
74.2.T49	Theology
74.2.T68	Tourist trade
	Travels, see 74.2.V68
74.2.V68	Voyages and travels
74.2.W37	War
	Textbooks for foreign speakers
74.3	Theory, methods, etc., for teachers
74.5	General
75.A-Z	By language, A-Z
	Phonology
	Including phonemics
	Cf. 89-97, Alphabet
76	General works
	Phonetics
77	General works
78	Palatalization
79	Pronunciation
81	Accent
81.3	Clitics
81.5	Intonation
81.7	Prosodic analysis
82	Phonetics of the sentence (Sandhi)
	Orthography. Spelling
83	History. General works
85	Spelling books
87	Spelling reform
88	Phonetic readers
	Alphabet
89	General works
90	Transliteration
91	Vowels
92	Diphthongs
93	Consonants
94	Contraction (Hiatis. Elision)

	Style. Composition.
	Rhetoric -- Continued
245	Textbooks
250	Outlines, questions, exercises, specimens. List of subjects
(251.A-Z)	Special authors, A-Z
	see the author in classes PA-PT
252	Discourse analysis
	Special parts of rhetoric
253	Style. Invention, narrative, etc.
255	Other special. Figures, tropes, allegory, etc.
256	Choice of words. Vocabulary, etc.
258	Punctuation
260	Idioms. Errors. Blunders
	Special classes of composition
263	Essays, lectures, newspaper style, precis writing, report writing, etc.
	Letter writing
265	General works
267	Specimens. Collections
	Translating
	For special subjects, see classes B-Z, e.g. T11.5, Technology
268	General works
269	Machine translating
	Including research
	Prosody. Metrics. Rhythmics
271	History of the science
	General works
274	Early to 1800
275	1800-
279	Textbooks
281	Versification (Gradus ad Parnassum)
283	Rhyme. Rhyming dictionaries
285.A-Z	Special. By form, A-Z
285.E6	Epic
285.L9	Lyric
290.A-Z	Special meters, A-Z
290.A3	Alexandrine
290.D4	Decasyllable
290.F8	Free verse
295	Other special
	Including epithets
(297)	Special authors
	see the author in classes PA-PT
298	Rhythm
299	Rhythm in prose
299.5	Lexicology
	Etymology
301	Treatises
302	Popular works

	Etymology -- Continued
303	Names (General)
	For personal names see CS2300 +, for place names, see G104 +, (General) or classes D - F for names of specific continents or countries
305	Dictionaries (exclusively etymological)
307.A-Z	Special elements. By language, A-Z
307.A3	Foreign elements (General)
	Cf. 343, Dictionaries
307.5	Other special
308	Folk etymology
310	Semantics
315	Synonyms. Antonyms. Paronyms. Homonyms
317	Onomatopoeic words
319.A-Z	Particular words, A-Z
	Lexicography
320	Periodicals. Societies. Serials. Collections (nonserial)
323	General works
	Biography of lexicographers, see 33-34
323.5	Criticism, etc., of particular dictionaries
	Dictionaries
	Dictionaries with definitions in same language
325	Early to 1800
	1800-
327	General
328	Picture dictionaries
329	Supplementary dictionaries. Dictionaries of new words
331	Dictionaries with definitions in two or more languages, or dictionaries of two or more languages with definitions in one language
333	Dictionaries with definitions in English
335.A-Z	Dictionaries with definitions in other languages. By language, A-Z
	Dictionaries exclusively etymological, see 305
337	Dictionaries of particular periods (other than periods separately specified elsewhere)
(339)	Dictionaries of particular authors
	see the author in classes PA-PT
341	Dictionaries of names
	Cf. 344, Foreign words
	Cf. CS2300 +, Genealogy
	Dictionaries, etc. of obsolete, archaic words and provincialisms
342	General works
	Local provincialisms, see 351-395
	Dictionaries of foreign words
343	General
344	Names
	Special. By language, see 307.A-Z
	Other special lists
345	Glossaries

1	Periodicals. Serials
3	Societies
	Collections (nonserial)
5	Texts, sources, etc.
	Class here only collections of texts
	For readers, see 37
	For texts and studies, see 7
7	Monographs. Studies
8.A-Z	Studies in honor of a particular person or institution, A-Z
9	Individual authors
11	Encyclopedias
12	Atlases, maps, charts, tables, etc.
	Cf. 192, Linguistic geography
13	Philosophy. Theory. Method. Relations
	History of philology
	Cf. 19-21.5, Study and teaching
	Cf. P-PZ3 25, History of the language
15	General works
	Biography, memoirs, etc.
17.A2	Collective
17.A5-Z	Individual, A-Z
	Study and teaching. Research
19	General works
20.A-Z	By region or country, A-Z
21.A-Z	By school, A-Z
21.5.A-A	By research institute, A-Z
	General works
22	Early to 1800
23	Treatises (Philology, General)
	General special
23.5	General works
24	Relation to other languages
24.5	Language data processing
24.7	Language standardization and variation
24.73	Political aspects
	Cf. 198.P6, Slang
24.75	Social aspects
24.8	Spoken language
24.85	Language acquisition
	History of the language
25	General works
	By region, see 187-199
26	Outlines
27	Popular
28	Script
	Grammar
29	Comparative (Two or more languages)
31	Historical
33	General works
34	General special
	Textbooks
35.A2	History and criticism

	Grammar
	Textbooks -- Continued
35.A3-Z	General textbooks
35.5	Self-instructors
35.7	Audiovisual instructors
	Readers
35.9	History and criticism
36	Series
37	Primers. Primary grade readers. Intermediate and advanced
37.3	Outlines, syllabi, tables, etc.
37.5	Examination questions, etc.
38.A-Z	Manuals for special classes of students, A-Z
38.C6	Commercial
	Cf. HF5719, Business report writing; HF5721, Business correspondence
38.F37	Farmers
38.F58	Fishermen
38.G35	Gardeners
38.L52	Library employees
38.M3	Medical personnel
38.M87	Musicians. Musicologists
38.P45	Personnel department employees
38.P47	Petroleum workers
38.P64	Police
38.P76	Professionals (General)
38.R4	Restaurant personnel
38.S34	School employees
	Self-instructors, see 35.5
38.S45	Servants
38.S57	Social workers
38.S58	Soldiers
38.T42	Technical
39	Conversation. Phrase books
	Idioms, errors, etc., see 145
39.15.A-Z	Readers on special subjects, A-Z
39.15.A45	Africa
39.15.A46	Africa, North
39.15.A7	Art
39.15.B5	Biography
39.15.C5	Civilization
39.15.C6	Commerce
39.15.C8	Current events
39.15.D48	Detective and mystery stories
39.15.D7	Drama
39.15.E25	Economics
39.15.E38	Education
39.15.E83	Ethnology
39.15.F35	Fantastic fiction
39.15.F54	Finance
39.15.F66	Folk literature
39.15.F7	France
39.15.G4	Geography

	Grammar
	Readers on special
	subjects, A-Z -- Continued
39.15.G44	Geology
39.15.H48	Hispanic Americans
39.15.H5	History
39.15.I8	Israel
39.15.I85	Italy
39.15.J35	Japan
39.15.J68	Journalism
39.15.L34	Latin America
39.15.L37	Law
39.15.L4	Legends
39.15.L45	Lermontov, Mikhail IU r'evich, 1814-1841
	Literature
	see P-PZ3 36-37
39.15.M3	Mathematics
39.15.M38	Medicine
39.15.M39	Mexican-Americans
39.15.M4	Mexico
39.15.M48	Military art and science
39.15.M5	Minorities
39.15.M87	Music
	Mystery stories, see 39.15.D48
39.15.N26	Names
39.15.N27	National characteristics
39.15.N3	Naval science
39.15.N48	New Mexico
39.15.N49	Newspapers
39.15.O33	Occupations
39.15.P45	Philosophy
39.15.P48	Physics
39.15.P63	Poetry
39.15.P64	Poland
39.15.P66	Political science
39.15.P8	Public administration
39.15.P87	Pushkin, Aleksandr Sergeevich, 1799-1837
39.15.R34	Railroads
39.15.R86	Russian history
39.15.S4	Science
39.15.S6	Social sciences
	Soviet history, see 39.15.R86
39.15.S63	Spain
39.15.T47	Theater
39.15.T49	Theology
39.15.T68	Tourist trade
	Travels, see 39.15.V68
39.15.V68	Voyages and travels
39.15.W37	War
	Textbooks for foreign speakers
39.2	Theory, methods, etc., for teachers
39.3	General
39.5.A-Z	By language, A-Z

	Grammar -- Continued
	Phonology
	Including phonemics
	Cf. 51-57, Alphabet
40	General works
	Phonetics
41	General works
42	Palatalization
43	Pronunciation
44	Accent
44.3	Clitics
44.5	Intonation
44.7	Prosodic analysis
44.9	Phonetics of the sentence (Sandhi)
	Orthography. Spelling
45	History. General works
47	Spelling books
49	Spelling reform
50	Phonetic readers
	Alphabet
51	General works
52	Transliteration
53	Vowels
54	Diphthongs
55	Consonants
56	Contraction (Hiatis. Elision)
57	Particular letters
58	Syllabication
	Punctuation, see 143
58.5	Capitalization
58.9	Morphophonemics
	Morphology
59	General works
61	Word formation
	Inflection
62	General works
(63)	Noun. Declension
	see P-PZ3 71-75
(65)	Adjective. Adverb. Comparison
	see P-PZ3 77-79
(67)	Verb. Conjugation
	see P-PZ3 85-99
69	Tables. Paradigms
	Parts of speech (Morphology and Syntax)
70	General works
70.5	Parsing
	Noun
71	General works
73	Gender. Number
75	Case
	Adjective. Adverb. Comparison
77	General works
79	Numerals

	Grammar
	Parts of speech (Morphology
	and Syntax) -- Continued
81	Article
83	Pronoun
	Verb
85	General works
87	Person
88	Number
89	Voice
91	Mood
95	Tense
95.5	Aspects of verbal action
96	Infinitive and participle
	Including gerund
97.A-Z	Special classes of verbs, A-Z
97.A8	Auxiliary
97.F3	Factitive
97.I46	Imperative
97.I6	Impersonal
	Intransitive/Transitive, see 97.T4
97.I8	Irregular
97.P4	Periphrastic
97.P52	Phrasal
97.R4	Reflexive
97.T4	Transitive/Intransitive
98.A-Z	Particular verbs, A-Z
99	Other. Miscellaneous
	Particle
101	General works
103	Adverb
105	Preposition
106	Postposition
107	Conjunction
109	Interjection
111.A-Z	Other special, A-Z
111.C54	Clitics
111.N4	Negatives
	Syntax
	General
113	General works
115	Outlines
117	General special
	Sentences
119	General arrangement, etc.
121	Order of words
123	Order of clauses
125	Clauses
127	Other special
129.A-Z	Other aspects, A-Z
129.A35	Agreement
129.A52	Anaphora
129.A66	Apposition

	Grammar
	Other aspects, A-Z -- Continued
129.C38	Causative
129.C65	Complement
129.D42	Definiteness
129.D44	Deixis
129.D46	Dependency grammar
129.D47	Determiners
129.E95	Existential constructions
129.G73	Grammatical categories
129.H65	Honorific
129.I57	Interrogative
129.L62	Locative constructions
129.M63	Modality
129.T46	Temporal constructions
(131.A-Z)	Grammatical usage of particular authors, A-Z
	see the author in classes PA-PT
	Style. Composition. Rhetoric
	For study and teaching, see 19-21.5
135	General works
137	Textbooks
139	Outlines, questions, exercises and specimens. List of subjects
(140.A-Z)	Special authors, A-Z
	see the author in classes PA-PT
140.5	Discourse analysis
	Special parts of rhetoric
141	Style. Invention, narration, etc. Figures, tropes, allegory, etc.
142	Choice of words. Vocabulary, etc.
143	Punctuation
145	Idioms. Errors. Blunders
	Special classes of composition
147	Essays, lectures, newspaper style, precis writing, report writing, etc.
	Letter writing
149	General works
149.5	Specimens. Collections
	Translating
	For special subjects, see classes B-Z, e.g. T11.5, Technology
150	General works
150.5	Machine translating
	Including research
	Prosody. Metrics. Rhythmics
151	History of the science
	General works
152	Early to 1800
153	1800-
155	Textbooks
157	Versification (Gradus ad Parnassum)
158	Rhyme. Rhyming dictionaries
159.A-Z	Special forms, meters, etc., A-Z

	Prosody. Metrics.
	Rhythmics -- Continued
160	Rhythm. Rhythm in prose
160.5	Lexicology
	Etymology
161	Treatises
161.5	Popular works
162	Names (General)
	For personal names see CS2300+, for place names, see G104+, (General) or classes D - F for names of specific continents or countries
163	Dictionaries (exclusively etymological)
164.A-Z	Special elements. By language, A-Z
164.A3	Foreign elements (General)
	Cf. 184, Dictionaries
164.3	Other special
164.5	Folk etymology
165	Semantics
167	Synonyms. Antonyms. Paronyms. Homonyms
168	Onomatopoeic words
169.A-Z	Particular words, A-Z
	Lexicography
171	Periodicals. Societies. Serials. Collections (nonserial)
173	General works
	Biography of lexicographers, see 17.A2-Z
173.5	Criticism, etc., of particular dictionaries
	Dictionaries
	Dictionaries with definitions in same language
175	General
176	Picture dictionaries
177	Supplementary dictionaries. Dictionaries of new words
178	Dictionaries with definitions in two or more languages, or dictionaries of two or more languages with definitions in one language
179	Dictionaries with definitions in English
181.A-Z	Dictionaries with definitions in other languages. By language, A-Z
	Dictionaries exclusively etymological, see 163
182	Dictionaries of particular periods (other than periods separately specified elsewhere)
183	Dictionaries of names
	Cf. 184, Foreign words
	Cf. CS2300+, Genealogy
	Dictionaries, etc. of obsolete, archaic words and provincialisms, see 185
184	Dictionaries of foreign words
	For special languages, see 164.A-Z
185	Other special lists
	Including glossaries, dictionaries of terms and phrases, word frequency lists, reverse indexes, and lists of abbreviations

	Linguistic geography. Dialects, etc.
187.A1	Linguistic geography
	Cf. 192, Atlases
	Dialects, provincialisms, etc.
	For language standardization and variation, see 24.7
187.A2-A29	Periodicals. Collections
187.A3-Z	Collections of texts, etc.
188	General works
189	Grammar
191	Dictionaries
192	Atlases, maps, charts, tables
193.A-Z	Local. By region, place, etc., A-Z
	Slang. Argot
195	Collections
196	General works
197	Dictionaries. Lists
197.5	Texts
198.A-Z	Special topics, A-Z
198.B88	Butchers' language
198.C35	Cant
198.C6	Court and courtiers language
198.C84	Cultural property
198.N63	Nobility
198.O27	Obscene words
198.O65	Opera production
198.P6	Political language
198.R3	Railroad language
198.S64	Soldiers' language
198.S66	Sports language
198.S82	Students' language
198.W65	Women's language
198.W67	World War II
198.Y68	Youth
199.A-Z	Special local, A-Z

1	Periodicals. Serials. Annuals. Yearbooks. Societies
2	Collections (nonserial)
3	Encyclopedias
4	Atlases, maps, charts, tables
	Cf. 98.A1, Linguistic geography
5	Philosophy. Theory. Method. Relations
	History of philology
	Cf. 11, Study and teaching
	Cf. 15, History of the language
7	General works
	Biography, memoirs, etc.
9.A2	Collective
9.A5-Z	Individual, A-Z
11	Study and teaching. Research
	General works
13	Treatises (Philology, General)
14	General special
14.7	Language standardization and variation
14.85	Language acquisition
	History of the language
15	General works
	By region, see 96-99
16	Outlines
17	Popular
17.5	Script
	Grammar
18	Comparative (Two or more languages)
19	Historical
21	General works
22	General special
	Textbooks
23.A2	History and criticism
23.A3-Z	General textbooks
23.5	Self-instructors
23.7	Audio-visual instructors
	Readers
23.9	History and criticism
24	Series
25	Primers. Primary grade readers. Intermediate and advanced
25.3	Outlines, syllabi, tables, etc.
25.5	Examination questions, etc.
26.A-Z	Manuals for special classes of students, A-Z
26.C6	Commercial
	Cf. HF5719, Business report writing; HF5721, Business correspondence
26.F37	Farmers
26.F58	Fishermen
26.G35	Gardeners
26.L52	Library employees
26.M3	Medical personnel
26.M87	Musicians. Musicologists
26.P45	Personnel department employees

	Grammar
	Manuals for special
	classes of students, A-Z -- Continued
26.P47	Petroleum workers
26.P64	Police
26.P76	Professionals (General)
26.R4	Restaurant personnel
26.S34	School employees
	Self-instructors, see 23.5
26.S45	Servants
26.S57	Social workers
26.S58	Soldiers
26.T42	Technical
27	Conversation. Phrase books
	Idioms, errors, etc., see 79
27.15.A-Z	Readers on special subjects, A-Z
27.15.A45	Africa
27.15.A46	Africa, North
27.15.A7	Art
27.15.B5	Biography
27.15.C5	Civilization
27.15.C6	Commerce
27.15.C8	Current events
27.15.D48	Detective and mystery stories
27.15.D7	Drama
27.15.E25	Economics
27.15.E38	Education
27.15.E83	Ethnology
27.15.F35	Fantastic fiction
27.15.F54	Finance
27.15.F66	Folk literature
27.15.F7	France
27.15.G4	Geography
27.15.G44	Geology
27.15.H48	Hispanic Americans
27.15.H5	History
27.15.I8	Israel
27.15.I85	Italy
27.15.J35	Japan
27.15.J68	Journalism
27.15.L34	Latin America
27.15.L37	Law
27.15.L4	Legends
27.15.L45	Lermontov, Mikhail IUr'evich, 1814-1841
	Literature
	see P-PZ4 24-25
27.15.M3	Mathematics
27.15.M38	Medicine
27.15.M39	Mexican-Americans
27.15.M4	Mexico
27.15.M48	Military art and science
27.15.M5	Minorities
27.15.M87	Music

	Grammar
	Readers on special
	subjects, A-Z -- Continued
	Mystery stories, see 27.15.D48
27.15.N26	Names
27.15.N27	National characteristics
27.15.N3	Naval science
27.15.N48	New Mexico
27.15.N49	Newspapers
27.15.O33	Occupations
27.15.P45	Philosophy
27.15.P48	Physics
27.15.P63	Poetry
27.15.P64	Poland
27.15.P66	Political science
27.15.P8	Public administration
27.15.P87	Pushkin, Aleksandr Sergeevich, 1799-1837
27.15.R34	Railroads
27.15.R86	Russian history
27.15.S4	Science
27.15.S6	Social sciences
	Soviet history, see 27.15.R86
27.15.S63	Spain
27.15.T47	Theater
27.15.T49	Theology
27.15.T68	Tourist trade
	Travels, see 27.15.V68
27.15.V68	Voyages and travels
27.15.W37	War
	Textbooks for foreign speakers
27.2	Theory, methods, etc., for teachers
27.3	General
27.5.A-Z	By language, A-Z
	Phonology
	Including phonemics
	Cf. 37, Alphabet
28	General works
	Phonetics
29	General works
30	Palatalization
31	Pronunciation
32	Accent
32.3	Clitics
32.5	Intonation
32.7	Prosodic analysis
32.9	Phonetics of the sentence (Sandhi)
	Orthography. Spelling
33	History. General works
35	Spelling books
36	Phonetic readers
37	Alphabet
	Including vowels, consonants, etc.
38	Morphophonemics

	Grammar -- Continued
	Morphology
39	General works
40	Word formation
	Inflection
41	General works
(42)	Noun. Declension
	see P-PZ4 49
(43)	Adjective. Adverb. Comparison
	see P-PZ4 53-55
(45)	Verb. Conjugation
	see P-PZ4 61-66.5
47	Tables. Paradigms
	Parts of speech (Morphology and Syntax)
48	General works
48.5	Parsing
49	Noun
	Adjective. Adverb. Comparison
53	General works
55	Numerals
57	Article
59	Pronoun
	Verb
61	General works
64	Person. Number. Voice. Mood. Tense. Aspects of verbal action. Infinitive and participle. Gerund
65.A-Z	Special classes of verbs, A-Z
65.A8	Auxiliary
65.F3	Factitive
65.I46	Imperative
65.I6	Impersonal
	Intransitive/Transitive, see 65.T72
65.I8	Irregular
65.P4	Periphrastics
65.P52	Phrasal
65.R4	Reflexive
65.T72	Transitive/Intransitive
66.A-Z	Particular verbs, A-Z
66.5	Other. Miscellaneous
67	Particle
71	Syntax
72.A-Z	Other aspects, A-Z
72.A52	Anaphora
72.A66	Apposition
72.C38	Causative
72.C65	Complement
72.D42	Definiteness
72.D44	Deixis
72.D46	Dependency grammar
72.D47	Determiners
72.E95	Existential constructions
72.G73	Grammatical categories

	Grammar
	Other aspects, A-Z -- Continued
72.H65	Honorific
72.I57	Interrogative
72.L62	Locative constructions
72.M63	Modality
72.T46	Temporal constructions
(73.A-Z)	Grammatical usage of particular authors, A-Z
	see the author in classes PA-PT
	Style. Composition. Rhetoric
	For study and teaching, see 11
75	General works
79	Idioms. Errors. Blunders
80	Special classes of composition
80.5	Translating
	For special subjects, see classes B-Z, e.g. T11.5,
	Technology
81	Prosody. Metrics. Rhythmics
82	Lexicology
	Etymology
83	Treatises
83.3	Names (General)
	For personal names see CS2300 +, for place names, see
	G104 +, (General) or classes D - F for names of
	specific continents or countries
83.5	Dictionaries (exclusively etymological)
84.A-Z	Special elements. By language, A-Z
84.A3	Foreign elements (General)
84.3	Other special
84.5	Folk etymology
85	Semantics
86	Synonyms. Antonyms. Paronyms. Homonyms
86.5	Onomatopoeic words
86.9.A-Z	Particular words, A-Z
	Lexicography
87	General works
	For biography of lexicographers, see 9.A2-Z
	Dictionaries
89	Dictionaries with definitions in same language
90	Dictionaries with definitions in two or more
	languages, or dictionaries of two or more
	languages with definitions in one language
91	Dictionaries with definitions in English
93.A-Z	Dictionaries with definitions in other languages.
	By language, A-Z
	Dictionaries exclusively etymological, see 83.5
93.2	Dictionaries of particular periods (other than
	periods separately specified elsewhere)
95	Other special lists
	Linguistic geography. Dialects, etc.
96.A1	Linguistic geography
	Cf. 98.A1, Atlases

	Linguistic geography.
	Dialects, etc. -- Continued
	Dialects, provincialisms, etc.
	For language standardization and variation, see 14.7
96.A2-A29	Periodicals. Collections
96.A3	Collections of texts, etc.
96.A5-Z	General works. Grammar
97	Dictionaries
98.A1	Atlases, maps, charts, tables. By date
98.A5-Z	Local. By region, place, etc., A-Z
99	Slang. Argot

1	Periodicals. Serials. Annuals. Yearbooks. Societies
2	Collections (nonserial)
3	Encyclopedias
4	Philosophy. Theory. Method. Relations
	History of philology
	Cf. 7, Study and teaching
	Cf. 9, History of the language
5	General works
	Biography, memoirs, etc.
6.A2	Collective
6.A5-Z	Individual, A-Z
7	Study and teaching. Research
	General works
8	Treatises (Philology, General)
8.5	Language data processing
8.8	Language standardization and variation. Spoken language. Language acquisition
	History of the language
9	General works
	By region, see 41.A1-46
9.5	Outlines
10	Popular
10.5	Script
	Grammar
11	General works
12	General special
	Textbooks
13.A2	History and criticism
13.A3-Z	Textbooks
	Including readers
15	Phonology
	Including phonemics and phonetics
	Cf. 18, Alphabet
17	Orthography. Spelling
18	Alphabet
18.9	Morphophonemics
19	Morphology
21	Parts of speech (Morphology and Syntax)
23	Syntax
25.A-Z	Other aspects, A-Z
25.A35	Agreement
25.A52	Anaphora
25.A66	Apposition
25.C38	Causative
25.C65	Complement
25.D42	Definiteness
25.D46	Dependency grammar
25.D47	Determiners
25.E95	Existential constructions
25.G73	Grammatical categories
25.H65	Honorific
25.I57	Interrogative
25.L62	Locative constructions

	Grammar
	Other aspects, A-Z -- Continued
25.M63	Modality
25.T46	Temporal constructions
(26.A-Z)	Grammatical usage of particular authors, A-Z
	see the author in classes PA-PT
27	Style. Composition. Rhetoric
	For study and teaching, see 7
28	Translating
	For special subjects, see classes B-Z, e.g. T11.5,
	Technology
29	Prosody. Metrics. Rhythmics
30	Lexicology
	Etymology
31	General treatises. Dictionaries
32	Semantics
33	Synonyms. Antonyms. Paronyms. Homonyms
33.5	Onomatopoeic words
33.9.A-Z	Particular words, A-Z
	Lexicography
34	General works
	Dictionaries
35	Dictionaries with definitions in same language
36	Dictionaries with definitions in two or more
	languages, or dictionaries of two or more
	languages with definitions in one language
37.A-Z	Dictionaries with definitions in English or other
	languages. By language, A-Z
	Dictionaries exclusively etymological, see 31
38	Dictionaries of particular periods (other than
	periods separately specified elsewhere)
39	Other special lists
	Linguistic geography. Dialects, etc.
41.A1	Linguistic geography
	Cf. 45.A1, Atlases
	Dialects, provincialisms, etc.
	For language standardization and variation, see 8.8
41.A2-A29	Periodicals. Collections
41.A3	Collections of texts, etc.
41.A5-Z	General works. Grammar
43	Dictionaries
45.A1	Atlases, maps, charts, tables. By date
45.A5-Z	Local. By region, place, etc., A-Z
46	Slang. Argot

1	Periodicals. Societies. Serials. Collections (nonserial)
2	Congresses
3	History of philology
5	Study and teaching
6	General works
7	History of the language
8	Script
	Grammar
9	General works
11	Phonology
12	Transliteration
13	Morphology
14	Parts of speech
15	Syntax
17	Style. Composition. Rhetoric
18	Translating
19	Prosody. Metrics. Rhytmmics
20	Lexicology
21	Etymology
	Lexicography
23	Dictionaries with definitions in the same language
25	Dictionaries with definitions in English and other languages
26	Lists of words
	Dialects
27	General works
28.A-Z	Special. By name or place, A-Z
29	Slang. Argot

1	General works
2	Grammar
5	Etymology. Lexicography. Dictionaries
7	Miscellaneous
9	Texts and commentaries

1.A1-A5	Periodicals. Societies. Serials. Collections
	(nonserial)
1.A6-Z	General works
2	General special (Script)
	Grammar. Treatises. Textbooks
3	Western
4	Oriental and other non-Western
5	Exercises. Readers. Phrase books, etc.
	Dictionaries
6	Western
7	Oriental and other non-Western
8	Literature (Table P-PZ25)
9	Other special
	e.g. Etymology
	Dialects
9.4	General works
9.5.A-Z	Special. By name or place, A-Z

1	Periodicals. Societies. Serials. Collections (nonserial)
2	General works
3	Grammar
4	Dictionaries
5	Texts

	Language
1	General works
2	Grammar
3	Dictionaries
	Literature
3.5	History
4.A2	Collections
	For language groups use P-PZ11 4.A2-4.Z5, for collections and omit numbers for individual authors
4.A3-Z5	Individual authors or works, A-Z (Table P-PZ40 or P-PZ43)
	Under language groups do not use these numbers for individual authors. See note under P-PZ11 4.A2
	Dialects
4.Z8	General works
4.Z9A-Z	Local. By dialect name or place, A-Z
	For language groups use local number for works too general to be classed with an individual language or separately classed smaller group
4.Z95A-Z	Translations into foreign languages, A-Z
	Subarrange by date

1	Periodicals. Societies. Serials. Collections (nonserial)
2	General works
3	General special
4	Grammar
5	Metrics
6	Etymology. Lexicography. Dictionaries
7.A-Z	Local. By dialect name or place, A-Z
	For language groups use local number for works too general to be classed with an individual language or separately classed smaller group
8	Texts

1.A1-A5	Periodicals. Societies. Serials. Collections (nonserial)
1.A6-Z	General works. Grammar
2	Dictionaries
3	Texts
4.A-Z9	Local. By dialect name or place, A-Z
	For language groups use local number for works too general to be classed with an individual language or separately classed smaller group
4.Z95A-Z	Translations into foreign languages, A-Z
	Subarrange by date

0.A1-A5	Periodicals. Societies. Serials. Collections (nonserial)
0.A6-Z3	General works. Grammar
0.Z5	Dictionaries
0.Z77	Texts
0.Z9A-Z	Local. By dialect name or place, A-Z

0.Z9A-Z: For language groups use local number for works too general to be classed with an individual language or separately classed smaller group

0.Z95A-Z	Translations into foreign languages, A-Z

Subarrange by date

	Language
0	General works
0.1	Grammar
0.2	Exercises. Readers. Phrase books, etc.
0.25	Style. Composition. Rhetoric
0.3	Etymology
0.4	Dictionaries
	Literature
0.5	History
	Collections
	Including translations
0.6	General
0.7	Poetry
0.74	Drama
0.76	Prose
(0.8)	Folk literature
	see subclass GR
0.9A-Z	Individual authors or works, A-Z (Table P-PZ40 or P-PZ43)
	Dialects
0.94	General works
0.95A-Z	Special. By name or place, A-Z

	In this table, "x" represents either a decimal number or a Cutter number. Substitute the language or dialect number for "x" in the table, e.g. PL5439.27, Simelungun poetry; PL65.K57, Kirghiz poetry
	Language
.x	General works
.x1	Grammar
.x2	Exercises. Readers. Phrase books, etc.
.x25	Style. Composition. Rhetoric
.x3	Etymology
.x4	Dictionaries
	Literature
.x5	History
	Collections
	Including translations
.x6	General
.x7	Poetry
.x74	Drama
.x76	Prose
(.x8)	Folk literature
	see subclass GR
.x9A-Z	Individual authors or works, A-Z
	For decimal number languages only, subarrange individual authors by Table P-PZ40 and individual works by Table P-PZ43
	For Cutter number languages, do not apply tables for individual authors or works
	Dialects
.x94	General works
.x95A-Z	Special. By name or place, A-Z

	History and criticism
	Periodicals. Societies. Serials
0	Periodicals
1	Yearbooks
2	Societies
3	Congresses
3.5	Museums. Exhibitions
	Collected works (nonserial)
4	Several authors
5	Individual authors
6	Encyclopedias. Dictionaries
	Study and teaching
8	General works
9.A-Z	Individual schools. By name, A-Z
	Biography of scholars, teachers, etc.
9.4	Collective
9.5.A-Z	Individual, A-Z
	History
	General works
10	Early works
	Modern treatises
11	General works
12	Textbooks
13	Outlines, syllabi, quizzes, etc.
14	Addresses, essays, lectures
17	Awards, prizes (not A-Z)
18	Relation to history, civilization, culture, etc.
	Relation to other literatures
19	General works
20	Translations (as a subject)
21	Foreign authors (General)
	Treatment of special subjects, classes, etc.
22.A-Z	Subjects, A-Z
22.A37	Adventure
22.A54	Anger
22.A73	Argentina
22.A94	Autobiography
22.B83	Buenos Aires (Argentina)
22.C47	Childhood
22.C57	Cities and towns
22.C7	Crime
22.D43	Decadence
22.E38	Egypt
22.E93	Exiles
22.F35	Fantasy
22.F76	Frontier and pioneer life
22.G76	Grotesque
22.I73	Italy
22.L35	Landscape
22.M6	Modernism
22.N27	Nationalism
22.N3	Nature
22.P36	Papua New Guinea

	History and criticism
	History
	Treatment of special
	subjects, classes, etc.
	Subjects, A-Z -- Continued
22.P57	Periodization
22.P65	Popular literature
22.R36	Regionalism
22.R4	Religion
22.R45	Revolution
22.S6	Social problems
22.T3	Tango (Dance)
22.T73	Travel
22.W36	War
22.W45	The West
23.A-Z	Classes, A-Z
23.A1	Characters (General)
23.A8	Australian aborigines
23.B57	Blacks
23.C47	Children
23.G3	Gauchos
23.I45	Immigrants
23.I5	Indians, American
23.J4	Jews
23.P66	Poor
23.P7	Priests
23.P75	Prisoners
23.W6	Women
25.A-Z	Individual characters, A-Z
25.G35	Gandhi, Mahatma, 1869-1948
	Biography
27	Collective
	By period, see 35-55
	Individual, see 196-198.36
29	Memoirs, letters, etc.
31	Literary landmarks. Homes and haunts of authors
33	Women authors. Literary relations of women
34.A-Z	Other classes of authors, A-Z
34.A74	Asian
34.A96	Australian aborigines
34.B57	Black
34.G38	Gauchos
34.G39	Gays
34.G47	German
34.G73	Greeks
34.H56	Hispanic
34.I82	Italian
34.J48	Jewish
34.M44	Men
34.M45	Mennonites
34.M55	Minorities
34.P76	Protestant
34.S66	South Asian

	History and criticism
	Other classes
	of authors, A-Z -- Continued
34.W45	White
	By period
35	Origins
	Medieval
38	General works
39	Addresses, essays, lectures
40	Special subjects (not A-Z)
	Modern
	Renaissance
44	General works
45	Addresses, essays, lectures
46	Special subjects (not A-Z)
	16th-18th century
47	General works
48	Addresses, essays, lectures
49	Special subjects (not A-Z)
	19th century
50	General works
51	Addresses, essays, lectures
52	Special subjects (not A-Z)
	20th century
53	General works
54	Addresses, essays, lectures
55	Special subjects (not A-Z)
	Poetry
61	General works
	Medieval, see 38-40
	Modern
67	16th-18th century
69	(18th and) 19th century
71	20th century
	Special forms or subjects
77	Epic
79	Lyric
80	Popular poetry. Ballads, etc.
81.A-Z	Other, A-Z
81.B83	Buenos Aires
81.C55	Children's poetry
81.C64	Concrete poetry
81.D42	Decimas
81.F36	Fantastic
81.H33	Haiku
81.I53	Indians
81.L68	Love
81.M87	Mysticism
81.P64	Political poetry
81.P72	Prayer
81.P76	Protest
81.R4	Religious poetry
81.T35	Tangos

	History and criticism
	Poetry
	Special forms or subjects
	Other, A-Z -- Continued
81.V54	Villancicos
81.W65	Women
	Drama
83	General works
85	Early to 1800
87	19th century
89	20th century
93.A-Z	Special forms, A-Z
93.C54	Children's plays
93.F6	Folk drama
93.P38	Pastoral drama
93.R33	Radio plays
93.Y67	Young adult drama
95.A-Z	Special subjects, A-Z
95.B53	Blacks
95.M93	Myth
95.P4	Peasants
95.P64	Politics
95.S67	Sports
95.S9	Symbolism
95.Y67	Young adults
	Prose. Fiction
97	General works
99	Early to 1800
101	19th century
103	20th century
104	Short stories
107.A-Z	Special topics, A-Z
107.A39	Adventure
107.A45	Alienation (Social psychology)
107.A53	Amazon River Region
107.A78	Art. Artists
107.A87	Australian aborigines
107.B53	Blacks
107.B83	Buenos Aires (Argentina)
107.C44	Children
107.C45	Children's stories
107.C58	Cities and towns
107.D4	Death
107.D48	Detective and mystery stories
107.E75	Erotic stories
107.E93	Exiles
107.E95	Existentialism
107.F23	Fables
107.F25	Family
107.F27	Fantastic fiction
107.F4	Feuilletons
107.G74	Grotesque
107.H5	Historical fiction

	History and criticism
	Prose. Fiction
	Special topics, A-Z -- Continued
107.I5	Immigrants
107.I54	Indians, American
107.I7	Ireland
107.I83	Italians
107.J48	Jews
107.L55	Lima (Peru)
107.M36	Maps
107.M68	Motion pictures
107.M87	Music
107.N37	National characteristics
107.N38	Nationalism
107.O43	Old age
107.O87	Outsiders
107.P37	Partition, Territorial
107.P53	Picaresque
107.P64	Political fiction
107.P66	Popular literature
107.P68	Power (Social sciences)
107.P7	Prairies
107.P74	Prisoners
107.P76	Protest fiction
107.P87	Purdah
107.R34	Race
107.R42	Realism
107.R43	Regionalism
107.S26	Santiago de Chile
107.S3	Scatology
107.S34	Science fiction
107.S46	Serialized fiction
107.S49	Sex
107.S6	Social classes
107.S63	Social problems
107.S78	Style
107.S8	Supernatural
107.S85	Symbolism
107.T55	Time
107.U86	Utopias
107.V56	Violence
107.W6	Women
	Other forms
109	Oratory
110	Diaries
111	Letters
113	Essays
115	Wit and humor
117	Miscellaneous
(121)	Folk literature
	see subclass GR
123	Juvenile literature
	For special genres, see the genre

	Collections
	Collections
130	Periodicals
133	Comprehensive collections
135	Selections. Anthologies
136.A-Z	Special classes of authors, A-Z
136.A47	Air pilots
136.A72	Arabs
136.A94	Australian aborigines
136.B55	Blacks
136.C5	Children
136.C54	Chinese
136.C6	College students
136.E84	Eskimos
136.E85	Exiles
136.G38	Gays
136.I5	Indians, American
136.I82	Italians
136.J48	Jews
136.L38	Lawyers
136.L47	Lesbians
136.M46	Mentally ill
136.M56	Minorities
136.P48	Physicians
136.P7	Prisoners
136.S3	School children
136.S69	South Asians
136.W6	Women
136.5.A-Z	Special topics, A-Z
136.5.B33	Bahai Faith
136.5.B37	Baseball
136.5.B83	Buenos Aires (Argentina)
136.5.C3	Canada
136.5.C33	Canadian Rockies
136.5.C36	Cats
136.5.C46	Children
136.5.C462	Chile saltpeter industry
136.5.C48	Christmas
136.5.C55	City and town life
136.5.C68	Country life
136.5.C75	Crime
136.5.D64	Dogs
136.5.D74	Drinking customs
136.5.E75	Erotic literature
136.5.F35	Family
136.5.F36	Fantasy
136.5.F45	Feminism
136.5.F57	Fire
136.5.F66	Food habits
136.5.F73	French-Canadians
136.5.F75	Frontier and pioneer life
136.5.G73	Grandmothers
136.5.G83	Guerrero, Vicente, 1782-1831
136.5.H47	Heroes

	Collections
	Special topics, A-Z -- Continued
136.5.H65	Homosexuality
136.5.H67	Horses
136.5.I45	Immigration
136.5.L35	Landscape
136.5.L37	Lapa (Rio de Janeiro, Brazil)
136.5.L53	Libraries. Librarians
136.5.L68	Love
136.5.M34	Mahabharata
136.5.M36	Maoris
136.5.M95	Mythology
136.5.N48	New literates
136.5.N54	Night
136.5.P4	Peace
136.5.P47	Peru Bolivian Confederation, 1836-1839
136.5.P64	Politics
136.5.P7	Prairies
136.5.P76	Protest literature
136.5.R68	Rosas, Juan Manuel José Domingo Ortiz de, 1793-1877
136.5.S35	Santiago del Estero (Argentina)
136.5.S36	Scotland
136.5.S65	Slavery
136.5.S66	Sports
136.5.S67	Spring
136.5.T33	Tabocas, Battle of, 1645
136.5.T72	Tramps
136.5.V55	Violence
136.5.V58	Vitória (Espírito Santo, Brazil)
136.5.W36	War
136.5.W38	Water
136.5.W66	Women
136.5.W67	World War, 1914-1918
137.A-Z	Translations. By language, A-Z
	By period
140	Medieval
141	16th-18th centuries
143	19th century
144	20th century
	Local, see 191-193
	Poetry
148	Periodicals
150	Comprehensive collections
151	Selections. Anthologies
152	Anthologies of poetry for children
	Special classes of authors
153	Women
154.A-Z	Other, A-Z
154.A8	Asians
154.A86	Australian aborigines
154.B55	Blacks
154.C5	Children
154.C6	College students. College verse

	Collections
	Poetry
	Special classes of authors
	Other, A-Z -- Continued
154.G68	Government employees
154.I53	Indians, American
154.I8	Italians
154.L33	Laboring classes
154.M45	Men
154.P7	Prisoners
154.S3	Students. School verse
154.V47	Veterinarians
	By period
155	Medieval
156	15th-18th century
157	19th century
158	20th century
	Special. By form or subject
160	Popular poetry. Ballads, etc.
161.A-Z	Other, A-Z
161.A35	Africa
161.A36	Aging
161.A5	Anchieta, Jose de 1534-1597
161.B55	Birds
161.B67	Borges, Jorge Luis, 1899-
161.B8	Buenos Aires
161.C18	Canada
161.C25	Capital punishment
161.C35	Christian poetry
161.C4	Christmas
161.C57	City and town life
	College verse, see 154.C6
161.C64	Concrete poetry
161.C83	Cuevas, José Luis, 1934-
161.D35	Death
161.D4	Descriptive poetry
161.D68	Down (Northern Ireland)
161.D72	Drug abuse
161.E35	Edinburgh (Scotland)
161.E5	Elegaic poetry
161.E52	England
161.E75	Erotic poetry
161.E95	Europe
161.F35	Falkland Islands
161.F36	Famines
161.F6	Fortaleza (Brazil)
161.F76	Frontier and pioneer life
161.G3	Gauchos
161.H25	Haiku
161.H4	Heart
161.H5	History
161.H57	Honor
161.H85	Humorous poetry

Collections
  Poetry
    Special. By form or subject
    Other, A-Z -- Continued

161.I53	Indians, American
161.I74	Irigoyen, Hipólito
161.J3	Jacobites
161.L3	Labor and laboring classes
161.L38	Lawyers
161.L6	Love
161.L8	Lyrics. Songs
161.M18	Maclean, John, 1879-1923
161.M62	Monterey (Mexico)
161.M64	Mother
161.N2	Narrative poetry
161.N64	Nonsense verse
161.O44	Olinda (Brazil)
161.O75	Orizaba, Mexico
161.P28	Paris (France)
161.P3	Patriotic poetry
161.P4	Peace
161.P59	Political poetry
161.P7	Prison life
161.P76	Protest poetry
161.Q3	Quatrains
161.Q43	Québec (Province)
161.R3	Railroads
161.R36	Rap
161.R39	Recife (Brazil)
161.R4	Religious poetry
161.R48	Revolutionary poetry
161.R53	Riel Rebellion, 1885
161.R59	Rizal y Alonso, Jose
161.S3	Satire
161.S4	Sea poetry
161.S57	Sonnets
161.S6	Spring
161.S77	Street children
161.T3	Tango (Dance)
161.T7	Trees
161.T86	Túpac-Amaru, José Gabriel, d. 1781
161.V45	Veracruz Llave (Mexico)
161.W37	War
161.W45	Whales
161.W56	Wine
161.W65	Work
161.W67	World War, 1914-1918
163.A-Z	Translations. By language, A-Z

  Drama

164	Comprehensive collections
165	Selections. Anthologies
165.5	Stories, plots, etc.
165.7.A-Z	Special classes of authors, A-Z

	Collections
	Drama
	Special classes
	of authors, A-Z -- Continued
165.7.A88	Australian aborigines
165.7.G38	Gays
165.7.W65	Women
	By period
166	To 1800
167	19th century
169	20th century
170.A-Z	Special (Tragedies, comedies, etc.), A-Z
170.A53	AIDS (Disease)
170.C48	Children's plays
170.C5	Christian drama
170.C53	Christmas plays
170.C57	Circus
170.I53	Indians of North America
170.O5	One-act plays
170.P3	Pastoral drama
170.R34	Radio plays
170.Y67	Young adult drama
171.A-Z	Translations. By language, A-Z
	Prose
173	General prose collections
174.A-Z	Special. By form or subject, A-Z
174.A96	Autobiographies
174.C48	Children
174.G83	Guadalajara (Mexico)
174.M67	Motherhood
174.T7	Travel
174.W65	Women
	Fiction
175	General collections
176	Short stories
176.2.A-Z	Special classes of authors, A-Z
176.2.C64	College students. College prose
176.2.G39	Gays
176.2.I53	Indians
176.2.J49	Jews
176.2.L44	Legislators
176.2.M37	Maoris
176.2.M45	Men
176.2.V58	Visually handicapped
176.2.W65	Women
176.3	Digests, synopses, etc.
176.5.A-Z	Special. By form or subject, A-Z
176.5.C57	Christmas stories
176.5.C58	City and town life
176.5.D43	Death
176.5.D48	Detective and mystery stories
176.5.E75	Erotic stories
176.5.F34	Family

	Collections
	Prose
	Fiction
	Special. By
	form or subject, A-Z -- Continued
176.5.F35	Fantastic fiction
176.5.F37	Fathers and sons
176.5.G37	Gays
176.5.G45	Ghost stories
176.5.H67	Horror tales
176.5.H85	Humorous stories
176.5.I47	Imposters and imposture
176.5.L3	Labor and laboring classes
176.5.L68	Love stories
176.5.M36	Man-woman relationships
176.5.M48	Mexican Revolution, 1910-1920
	Mystery stories, see 176.5.D48
176.5.P64	Political fiction
176.5.R45	Religion
176.5.S33	Science fiction
176.5.S43	Sea stories
176.5.S53	Sisters
176.5.S58	Soccer
176.5.S62	Social problems
176.5.S66	Sports stories
176.5.T7	Travel
176.5.V54	Violence
	Working class, see 176.5.L3
177.A-Z	Translations. By language, A-Z
179	Oratory
180	Diaries
181	Letters
183	Essays
185	Wit and humor
187	Miscellany
188.A-Z	Translations. By language, A-Z
(189)	Folk literature
	see subclass GR
	For folk poetry, see 160
	Local
191.A-Z	By region, province, county, etc., A-Z (Table P-PZ26)
192.A-Z	By city, A-Z (Table P-PZ26)
193.A-Z	Foreign countries, A-Z (Table P-PZ26)
	Individual authors, A-Z
196	To 1810/25
	Each author is subarranged by Table P-PZ40, unless otherwise specified
197	1810/25-1960
	Each author is subarranged by Table P-PZ40, unless otherwise specified
198-198.36	1961- (Table P-PZ29)
	Each author is subarranged by Table P-PZ40, unless otherwise specified

	History and criticism
0	Periodicals. Serials. Societies
0.1	Collected works (nonserial). Individual authors
0.2	Encyclopedias. Dictionaries
	Study and teaching
2.2	General works
2.3.A-Z	Individual schools. By name, A-Z
	Biography of scholars, teachers, etc.
2.7	Collective
3.A-Z	Individual, A-Z
	History
	General works
4.2	Early works
	Modern treatises
4.3	General works
4.4	Textbooks
4.5	Outlines, syllabi, quizzes, etc.
4.6	Addresses, essays, lectures
4.8.A-Z	Awards, prizes (not A-Z)
5.2	Relation to history, civilization, culture, etc.
	Relation to other literatures
5.3	General works
5.4	Translations (as a subject)
5.45	Foreign authors (General)
	Treatment of special subjects, classes, etc.
5.5.A-Z	Subjects, A-Z
5.5.A37	Adventure
5.5.A54	Anger
5.5.A73	Argentina
5.5.A94	Autobiography
5.5.B83	Buenos Aires (Argentina)
5.5.C47	Childhood
5.5.C57	Cities and towns
5.5.C7	Crime
5.5.D43	Decadence
5.5.E38	Egypt
5.5.E93	Exiles
5.5.F35	Fantasy
5.5.F76	Frontier and pioneer life
5.5.G76	Grotesque
5.5.I73	Italy
5.5.L35	Landscape
5.5.M6	Modernism
5.5.N27	Nationalism
5.5.N3	Nature
5.5.P36	Papua New Guinea
5.5.P57	Periodization
5.5.P65	Popular literature
5.5.R36	Regionalism
5.5.R4	Religion
5.5.R45	Revolution
5.5.S6	Social problems
5.5.T3	Tango (Dance)

	History and criticism
	History
	Treatment of special
	subjects, classes, etc.
	Subjects, A-Z -- Continued
5.5.T73	Travel
5.5.W36	War
5.5.W45	West (U.S.)
5.6.A-Z	Classes, A-Z
5.6.A1	Characters (General)
5.6.A8	Australian aborigines
5.6.B57	Blacks
5.6.C47	Children
5.6.G3	Gauchos
5.6.I45	Immigrants
5.6.I5	Indians, American
5.6.J4	Jews
5.6.P66	Poor
5.6.P7	Priests
5.6.P75	Prisoners
5.6.W6	Women
5.7.A-Z	Individual characters, A-Z
5.7.G35	Gandhi, Mahatma, 1869-1948
	Biography
6.2	Collective
	By period, see 9-9.6
	Individual, see 19-19.3
6.3	Memoirs, letters, etc.
7	Literary landmarks. Homes and haunts of authors
8	Women authors. Literary relations of women
8.2.A-Z	Other classes of authors, A-Z
8.2.A74	Asian
8.2.A96	Australian aborigines
8.2.B57	Black
8.2.G38	Gauchos
8.2.G39	Gays
8.2.G47	German
8.2.G73	Greeks
8.2.H56	Hispanic
8.2.I82	Italian
8.2.J48	Jewish
8.2.M44	Men
8.2.M45	Mennonites
8.2.M55	Minorities
8.2.P76	Protestant
8.2.S66	South Asian
8.2.W45	White
	By period
9	Origins. Medieval
	Modern
9.3	Renaissance
9.4	16th-18th century
9.5	19th century

	History and criticism
	By period
	Modern -- Continued
9.6	20th century
	Poetry
10.2	General works
	Medieval, see 9
	Modern
10.3	16th-18th century
10.4	(18th and) 19th century
10.5	20th century
	Special forms or subjects
10.6	Epic
10.7	Lyric
10.8	Popular poetry. Ballads, etc.
10.9.A-Z	Other, A-Z
10.9.B83	Buenos Aires
10.9.C55	Children's poetry
10.9.C64	Concrete poetry
10.9.D42	Decimas
10.9.F36	Fantastic
10.9.H33	Haiku
10.9.I53	Indians
10.9.L68	Love
10.9.M87	Mysticism
10.9.P64	Political poetry
10.9.P72	Prayer
10.9.P76	Protest
10.9.R4	Religious poetry
10.9.T35	Tangos
10.9.V54	Villancicos
10.9.W65	Women
	Drama
11.2	General works
11.3	Early to 1800
11.4	19th century
11.5	20th century
11.6.A-Z	Special forms, A-Z
11.6.C54	Children's plays
11.6.F6	Folk drama
11.6.P38	Pastoral drama
11.6.R33	Radio plays
11.6.Y67	Young adult drama
11.7.A-Z	Special subjects, A-Z
11.7.B53	Blacks
11.7.M93	Myth
11.7.P4	Peasants
11.7.P64	Politics
11.7.S67	Sports
11.7.S9	Symbolism
11.7.Y67	Young adults
	Prose. Fiction
12.2	General works

	History and criticism
	Prose. Fiction -- Continued
12.3	Early to 1800
12.4	19th century
12.5	20th century
12.52	Short stories
12.6.A-Z	Special topics, A-Z
12.6.A39	Adventure
12.6.A45	Alienation (Social psychology)
12.6.A53	Amazon River Region
12.6.A78	Art. Artists
12.6.A87	Australian aborigines
12.6.B53	Blacks
12.6.B83	Buenos Aires (Argentina)
12.6.C44	Children
12.6.C45	Children's stories
12.6.C58	Cities and towns
12.6.D4	Death
12.6.D48	Detective and mystery stories
12.6.E75	Erotic stories
12.6.E93	Exiles
12.6.E95	Existentialism
12.6.F23	Fables
12.6.F25	Family
12.6.F27	Fantastic fiction
12.6.F4	Feuilletons
12.6.G74	Grotesque
12.6.H5	Historical fiction
12.6.I5	Immigrants
12.6.I54	Indians, American
12.6.I7	Ireland
12.6.I83	Italians
12.6.J48	Jews
12.6.L55	Lima (Peru)
12.6.M36	Maps
12.6.M87	Music
12.6.N37	National characteristics
12.6.N38	Nationalism
12.6.O43	Old age
12.6.O87	Outsiders
12.6.P37	Partition, Territorial
12.6.P53	Picaresque
12.6.P64	Political fiction
12.6.P66	Popular literature
12.6.P68	Power (Social sciences)
12.6.P7	Prairies
12.6.P74	Prisoners
12.6.P76	Protest fiction
12.6.P87	Purdah
12.6.R34	Race
12.6.R42	Realism
12.6.R43	Regionalism
12.6.S26	Santiago de Chile

	History and criticism
	Prose. Fiction
	Special topics, A-Z -- Continued
12.6.S3	Scatology
12.6.S34	Science fiction
12.6.S46	Serialized fiction
12.6.S49	Sex
12.6.S6	Social classes
12.6.S63	Social problems
12.6.S78	Style
12.6.S8	Supernatural
12.6.S85	Symbolism
12.6.T55	Time
12.6.U86	Utopias
12.6.V56	Violence
12.6.W6	Women
	Other forms
13.2	Oratory
13.3	Diaries
13.4	Letters
13.5	Essays
13.6	Wit and humor
13.7	Miscellaneous
(13.8)	Folk literature
	see subclass GR
13.9	Juvenile literature
	For special genres, see the genre
	Collections
14	Periodicals
14.3	Comprehensive collections
14.4	Selections. Anthologies
14.5.A-Z	Special classes of authors, A-Z
14.5.A47	Air pilots
14.5.A72	Arabs
14.5.A94	Australian aborigines
14.5.B55	Blacks
14.5.C5	Children
14.5.C54	Chinese
14.5.C6	College students
14.5.E84	Eskimos
14.5.E85	Exiles
14.5.G38	Gays
14.5.I5	Indians, American
14.5.I82	Italians
14.5.J48	Jews
14.5.L38	Lawyers
14.5.L47	Lesbians
14.5.M46	Mentally ill
14.5.M56	Minorities
14.5.P48	Physicians
14.5.P7	Prisoners
14.5.S3	School children
14.5.S69	South Asians

	Collections
	Special classes
	of authors, A-Z -- Continued
14.5.W6	Women
14.52.A-Z	Special topics, A-Z
14.52.B33	Bahai Faith
14.52.B37	Baseball
14.52.B83	Buenos Aires (Argentina)
14.52.C3	Canada
14.52.C33	Canadian Rockies
14.52.C36	Cats
14.52.C46	Children
14.52.C462	Chile saltpeter industry
14.52.C48	Christmas
14.52.C55	City and town life
14.52.C68	Country life
14.52.C75	Crime
14.52.D64	Dogs
14.52.D74	Drinking customs
14.52.E75	Erotic literature
14.52.F35	Family
14.52.F36	Fantasy
14.52.F45	Feminism
14.52.F57	Fire
14.52.F66	Food habits
14.52.F73	French-Canadians
14.52.F75	Frontier and pioneer life
14.52.G73	Grandmothers
14.52.G83	Guerrero, Vicente, 1782-1831
14.52.H47	Heroes
14.52.H65	Homosexuality
14.52.H67	Horses
14.52.I45	Immigration
14.52.L35	Landscape
14.52.L37	Lapa (Rio de Janeiro, Brazil)
14.52.L53	Libraries. Librarians
14.52.L68	Love
14.52.M34	Mahabharata
14.52.M36	Maoris
14.52.M95	Mythology
14.52.N48	New literates
14.52.N54	Night
14.52.P4	Peace
14.52.P47	Peru Bolivian Confederation, 1836-1839
14.52.P64	Politics
14.52.P7	Prairies
14.52.P76	Protest literature
14.52.R68	Rosas, Juan Manuel José Domingo Oriz de, 1793-1877
14.52.S35	Santiago del Estero (Argentina)
14.52.S36	Scotland
14.52.S65	Slavery
14.52.S66	Sports
14.52.S67	Spring

	Collections
	Special topics, A-Z -- Continued
14.52.T33	Tabocas, Battle of, 1645
14.52.T72	Tramps
14.52.V55	Violence
14.52.V58	Vitória (Espírito Santo, Brazil)
14.52.W36	War
14.52.W38	Water
14.52.W66	Women
14.52.W67	World War, 1914-1918
14.55.A-Z	Translations. By language, A-Z
	By period
14.6	Medieval
14.7	16th-18th centuries
14.8	19th century
14.9	20th century
	Local, see 18.2-4
	Poetry
15.1	Periodicals
15.23	Comprehensive collections
15.25	Selections. Anthologies
15.27	Anthologies of poetry for children
	Special classes of authors
15.3	Women
15.35.A-Z	Other, A-Z
15.35.A8	Asians
15.35.A86	Australian aborigines
15.35.B55	Blacks
15.35.C5	Children
15.35.C6	College students. College verse
15.35.G68	Government employees
15.35.I53	Indians, American
15.35.I8	Italians
15.35.L33	Laboring classes
15.35.M45	Men
15.35.P7	Prisoners
15.35.S3	Students. School verse
15.35.V47	Veterinarians
	By period
15.4	Medieval
15.5	15th-18th century
15.6	19th century
15.7	20th century
	Special. By form or subject
15.8	Popular poetry. Ballads, etc.
15.85.A-Z	Other, A-Z
15.85.A35	Africa
15.85.A36	Aging
15.85.A5	Anchieta, Jose de, 1534-1597
15.85.B55	Birds
15.85.B67	Borges, Jorge Luis, 1899-
15.85.B8	Buenos Aires
15.85.C18	Canada

	Collections
	Poetry
	Special. By form or subject
	Other, A-Z -- Continued
15.85.C25	Capital punishment
15.85.C35	Christian poetry
15.85.C4	Christmas
15.85.C57	City and town life
	College verse, see 15.35.C6
15.85.C64	Concrete poetry
15.85.C83	Cuevas, José Luis, 1934-
15.85.D35	Death
15.85.D4	Descriptive poetry
15.85.D68	Down (Northern Ireland)
15.85.D72	Drug abuse
15.85.E35	Edinburgh (Scotland)
15.85.E5	Elegaic poetry
15.85.E52	England
15.85.E75	Erotic poetry
15.85.E95	Europe
15.85.F35	Falkland Islands
15.85.F36	Famines
15.85.F6	Fortaleza (Brazil)
15.85.F76	Frontier and pioneer life
15.85.G3	Gauchos
15.85.H25	Haiku
15.85.H4	Heart
15.85.H5	History
15.85.H57	Honor
15.85.H85	Humorous poetry
15.85.I53	Indians, American
15.85.I74	Irigoyen, Hipólito
15.85.J3	Jacobites
15.85.L3	Labor and laboring classes
15.85.L38	Lawyers
15.85.L6	Love
15.85.L8	Lyrics. Songs
15.85.M18	Maclean, John, 1879-1923
15.85.M62	Monterrey (Mexico)
15.85.M64	Mothers
15.85.N2	Narrative poetry
15.85.N64	Nonsense verse
15.85.O44	Olinda (Brazil)
15.85.O75	Orizaba (Mexico)
15.85.P28	Paris (France)
15.85.P3	Patriotic poetry
15.85.P4	Peace
15.85.P59	Political poetry
15.85.P7	Prison life
15.85.P76	Protest poetry
15.85.Q3	Quatrains
15.85.Q43	Québec (Province)
15.85.R3	Railroads

	Collections
	Poetry
	Special. By form or subject
	Other, A-Z -- Continued
15.85.R36	Rap
15.85.R39	Recife (Brazil)
15.85.R4	Religious poetry
15.85.R48	Revolutionary poetry
15.85.R53	Riel Rebellion, 1885
15.85.R59	Rizal y Alonso, Jose
15.85.S3	Satire
15.85.S4	Sea poetry
15.85.S57	Sonnets
15.85.S6	Spring
15.85.S77	Street children
15.85.T3	Tango (Dance)
15.85.T7	Trees
15.85.T86	Túpac-Amaru, José Gabriel, d. 1781
15.85.V45	Veracruz Llave (Mexico)
15.85.W37	War
15.85.W45	Whales
15.85.W56	Wine
15.85.W65	Work
15.85.W67	World War, 1914-1918
15.9.A-Z	Translations. By language, A-Z
	Drama
16.2	Comprehensive collections
16.3	Selections. Anthologies
16.35	Stories, plots, etc.
16.37.A-Z	Special classes of authors, A-Z
16.37.A88	Australian aborigines
16.37.G38	Gays
16.37.W65	Women
	By period
16.4	To 1800
16.5	19th century
16.6	20th century
16.7.A-Z	Special (Tragedies, comedies, etc.), A-Z
16.7.A53	AIDS (Disease)
16.7.C48	Children's plays
16.7.C5	Christian drama
16.7.C53	Christmas plays
16.7.C57	Circus
16.7.I53	Indians of North America
16.7.O5	One-act plays
16.7.P3	Pastoral drama
16.7.R34	Radio plays
16.7.Y67	Young adult drama
16.8.A-Z	Translations. By language, A-Z
	Prose
17.25	General prose collections
17.28.A-Z	Special. By form or subject, A-Z
17.28.A96	Autobiographies

	Collections
	Prose
	Special. By
	form or subject, A-Z -- Continued
17.28.C48	Children
17.28.G83	Guadalajara (Mexico)
17.28.M67	Motherhood
17.28.T7	Travel
17.28.W65	Women
	Fiction
17.3	General collections
17.32	Short stories
17.33.A-Z	Special classes of authors, A-Z
17.33.C64	College students. College prose
17.33.G39	Gays
17.33.I53	Indians
17.33.J49	Jews
17.33.L44	Legislators
17.33.M37	Maoris
17.33.M45	Men
17.33.V58	Visually handicapped
17.33.W65	Women
17.34	Digests, synopses, etc.
17.35.A-Z	Special. By form or subject, A-Z
17.35.C57	Christmas stories
17.35.C58	City and town life
17.35.D43	Death
17.35.D48	Detective and mystery stories
17.35.E75	Erotic stories
17.35.F34	Family
17.35.F35	Fantastic fiction
17.35.F37	Fathers and sons
17.35.G37	Gays
17.35.G45	Ghost stories
17.35.H67	Horror tales
17.35.H85	Humorous stories
17.35.I47	Imposters and imposture
17.35.L3	Labor and laboring classes
17.35.L44	Legislators
17.35.L68	Love stories
17.35.M36	Man-woman relationships
17.35.M48	Mexican Revolution, 1910-1920
	Mystery stories, see 17.35.D48
17.35.P64	Political fiction
17.35.R45	Religion
17.35.S33	Science fiction
17.35.S43	Sea stories
17.35.S53	Sisters
17.35.S58	Soccer
17.35.S62	Social problems
17.35.S66	Sports stories
17.35.T7	Travel
17.35.V54	Violence

	Collections
	Prose
	Fiction
	Special. By
	form or subject, A-Z -- Continued
	Working class, see 17.35.L3
17.36.A-Z	Translations. By language, A-Z
17.4	Oratory
17.5	Diaries
17.6	Letters
17.7	Essays
17.8	Wit and humor
17.9	Miscellany
17.92.A-Z	Translations. By language, A-Z
(17.95)	Folk literature
	see subclass GR
	For folk poetry, see 15.8
	Local
18.2.A-Z	By region, province, county, etc., A-Z (Table P-PZ26)
18.3.A-Z	By city, A-Z (Table P-PZ26)
18.4.A-Z	Foreign countries, A-Z (Table P-PZ26)
	Individual authors, A-Z
19	To 1810/25
	Each author is subarranged by Table P-PZ40, unless
	otherwise specified
19.2	1810/25-1960
	Each author is subarranged by Table P-PZ40, unless
	otherwise specified
19.3	1961-
	Each author is subarranged by Table P-PZ40, unless
	otherwise specified

	History and criticism
1	Periodicals. Societies. Serials. Collected works (nonserial)
2	Encyclopedias. Dictionaries
3	Study and teaching
	Biography of critics, historians, etc.
4	Collective
4.5.A-Z	Individual, A-Z
	History
5	General works
6	Addresses, essays, lectures
7	Relation to history, civilization, culture, etc.
	Relation to other literatures
8	General works
9	Translations (as subject)
10.A-Z	Treatment of special subjects, classes, etc., A-Z
10.A44	Allegory
10.A87	Authors
10.F64	Folklore
10.K87	Kurds
10.L6	Love
10.M96	Mythology
10.N37	Nationalism
10.P64	Politics
10.P68	Poverty
10.P7	Psychology
10.R38	Realism
10.R4	Religion
10.R65	Romanticism
10.S4	Sex
10.S44	Slavery
10.S63	Society and literature
10.S95	Symbolism
10.U53	United States
10.W37	War
10.W65	Women
10.Y66	Youth
13	Biography (Collected)
	By period
15	Origins
16	Modern
	Poetry
17	General works
	By period
18	To 1900
19	20th century
20	Special forms and topics (not A-Z)
21	Drama
23	Prose. Fiction
	Other forms
24	Oratory
25	Letters
26	Essays

	History and criticism
	History
	Other forms -- Continued
27	Wit and humor
28	Miscellaneous
(29)	Folk literature
	see subclass GR
30	Juvenile literature (General)
	For special genres, see the genre
	Local, see 47.A-Z
	Collections
31	Comprehensive collections
32	Selections. Anthologies
32.5.A-Z	Special classes of authors, A-Z
32.5.P6	Policemen
32.5.S6	Soldiers
32.5.W66	Women
	Poetry
34	General
35	Special forms and topics (not A-Z)
37	Drama
	Prose
39	General
40	Fiction
41	Oratory
42	Letters
43	Essays
44	Wit and humor
45	Miscellany
(46)	Folk literature
	see subclass GR
47.A-Z	Local, A-Z (Table P-PZ26)
48.A-Z	Individual authors or works, A-Z
	Each author subarranged by Table P-PZ40, unless otherwise specified

	History
0	Periodicals. Societies. Serials
0.15	Congresses
0.2	Encyclopedias. Dictionaries
0.3	Study and teaching
0.6.A-Z	Biography of critics, historians, etc., A-Z
1	General works
2	General special
3	Addresses, essays, lectures
4	Biography (Collective)
5	Origins
6	To 1800
7	19th century
8	20th century
10	Poetry
11	Drama
12	Other
	Collections
12.5	Periodicals
13	Collections
13.5.A-Z	Translations. By language, A-Z
	Poetry
14	Collections
14.5.A-Z	Translations. By language, A-Z
	Drama
15	Collections
15.5.A-Z	Translations. By language, A-Z
	Other
16	Collections
16.5.A-Z	Translations. By language, A-Z
17.A-Z	Local, A-Z (Table P-PZ26)
19.A-Z	Individual authors or works, A-Z
	Each author or work subarranged by Table P-PZ40 or P-PZ43, unless otherwise specified

	History
0.A1-A5	Periodicals. Societies. Serials
0.A515	Congresses
0.A52	Encyclopedias. Dictionaries
0.A53	Study and teaching
0.A56A-Z	Biography of critics, historians, etc., A-Z
0.A6-Z	General works
0.5	General special
1	Biography (Collective)
2	Poetry
3	Drama
4	Other
	Collections
4.5	Periodicals
5	Collections
5.5.A-Z	Translations. By language, A-Z
	Poetry
6	Collections
6.5.A-Z	Translations. By language, A-Z
	Drama
7	Collections
7.5.A-Z	Translations. By language, A-Z
	Other
8	Collections
8.2.A-Z	Translations. By language, A-Z
8.5.A-Z	Local, A-Z (Table P-PZ26)
9.A-Z	Individual authors or works, A-Z
	Each author or work subarranged by Table P-PZ40 or P-PZ42, unless otherwise specified

	History
0.A1-A5	Periodicals. Societies. Serials
0.A515	Congresses
0.A52	Encyclopedias. Dictionaries
0.A53	Study and teaching
0.A56A-Z	Biography of critics, historians, etc., A-Z
0.A6-Z	General works
0.05	General special
0.1	Biography (Collective)
0.2	Poetry
0.3	Drama
0.4	Other
	Collections
0.45	Periodicals
0.5	Collections
0.55.A-Z	Translations. By language, A-Z
	Poetry
0.6	Collections
0.65.A-Z	Translations. By language, A-Z
	Drama
0.7	Collections
0.75.A-Z	Translations. By language, A-Z
	Other
0.8	Collections
0.82.A-Z	Translations. By language, A-Z
0.85.A-Z	Local, A-Z (Table P-PZ26)
0.9.A-Z	Individual authors or works, A-Z
	Each author or work subarranged by Table P-PZ40 or P-PZ43, unless otherwise specified

	x = Cutter number
.x	History
.x2	Collections

	Works by unidentified authors are to be classed under the period to which they belong and are to precede the works of individual authors known by name, except as otherwise provided for in the schedule
0.A1A-Z	Works without any indication of author, either by symbol or initial. By title, A-Z
0.A2A-Z	Works by authors indicated by non-alphabetic symbols (dots, dashes, asterisks, etc.). By title, A-Z
0.A6A-Z	Works by authors indicated by a descriptive phrase. By first word of phrase, A-Z e.g.: PQ2149.A6I5, (Un) Ingenieur en chef honoraire des mines
0.A7	Works "By author of" arranged by the title named e.g.: PT1799.A7R8+, By the author of "Ruinen aus den sagen des nordens"
	Works by authors indicated by initials
0.A9	Works by A (single initial or supposed surname initial) Subarrange in one alphabet by title of work, disregarding symbols, words, or other initials that may be added
0.B3	Works by B (single initial or supposed surname initial) Subarrange in one alphabet by title of work, disregarding symbols, words, or other initials that may be added
0.C3	Works by C (single initial or supposed surname initial) Subarrange in one alphabet by title of work, disregarding symbols, words, or other initials that may be added
0.D3	Works by D (single initial or supposed surname initial) Subarrange in one alphabet by title of work, disregarding symbols, words, or other initials that may be added
0.E3	Works by E (single initial or supposed surname initial) Subarrange in one alphabet by title of work, disregarding symbols, words, or other initials that may be added
0.F3	Works by F (single initial or supposed surname initial) Subarrange in one alphabet by title of work, disregarding symbols, words, or other initials that may be added
0.G3	Works by G (single initial or supposed surname initial) Subarrange in one alphabet by title of work, disregarding symbols, words, or other initials that may be added

	Works by authors
	indicated by initials -- Continued
0.H3	Works by H (single initial or supposed surname initial)
	Subarrange in one alphabet by title of work, disregarding symbols, words, or other initials that may be added
0.I3	Works by I (single initial or supposed surname initial)
	Subarrange in one alphabet by title of work, disregarding symbols, words, or other initials that may be added
0.J3	Works by J (single initial or supposed surname initial)
	Subarrange in one alphabet by title of work, disregarding symbols, words, or other initials that may be added
0.K3	Works by K (single initial or supposed surname initial)
	Subarrange in one alphabet by title of work, disregarding symbols, words, or other initials that may be added
0.L3	Works by L (single initial or supposed surname initial)
	Subarrange in one alphabet by title of work, disregarding symbols, words, or other initials that may be added
0.M3	Works by M (single initial or supposed surname initial)
	Subarrange in one alphabet by title of work, disregarding symbols, words, or other initials that may be added
0.N3	Works by N (single initial or supposed surname initial)
	Subarrange in one alphabet by title of work, disregarding symbols, words, or other initials that may be added
0.O3	Works by O (single initial or supposed surname initial)
	Subarrange in one alphabet by title of work, disregarding symbols, words, or other initials that may be added
0.P3	Works by P (single initial or supposed surname initial)
	Subarrange in one alphabet by title of work, disregarding symbols, words, or other initials that may be added
0.Q3	Works by Q (single initial or supposed surname initial)
	Subarrange in one alphabet by title of work, disregarding symbols, words, or other initials that may be added

Works by authors
    indicated by initials -- Continued
0.R3   Works by R (single initial or supposed surname
            initial)
              Subarrange in one alphabet by title of work,
                disregarding symbols, words, or other initials
                that may be added
0.S3   Works by S (single initial or supposed surname
            initial)
              Subarrange in one alphabet by title of work,
                disregarding symbols, words, or other initials
                that may be added
0.T3   Works by T (single initial or supposed surname
            initial)
              Subarrange in one alphabet by title of work,
                disregarding symbols, words, or other initials
                that may be added
0.U3   Works by U (single initial or supposed surname
            initial)
              Subarrange in one alphabet by title of work,
                disregarding symbols, words, or other initials
                that may be added
0.V3   Works by V (single initial or supposed surname
            initial)
              Subarrange in one alphabet by title of work,
                disregarding symbols, words, or other initials
                that may be added
0.W3   Works by W (single initial or supposed surname
            initial)
              Subarrange in one alphabet by title of work,
                disregarding symbols, words, or other initials
                that may be added
0.X3   Works by X (single initial or supposed surname
            initial)
              Subarrange in one alphabet by title of work,
                disregarding symbols, words, or other initials
                that may be added
0.Y3   Works by Y (single initial or supposed surname
            initial)
              Subarrange in one alphabet by title of work,
                disregarding symbols, words, or other initials
                that may be added
0.Z3   Works by Z (single initial or supposed surname
            initial)
              Subarrange in one alphabet by title of work,
                disregarding symbols, words, or other initials
                that may be added

0.A-Z		Anonymous works. By title, A-Z
0.1	A	

The author number is determined by the second letter
of the name

Each author is subarranged by Table P-PZ40, unless
otherwise specified

0.12	B	

The author number is determined by the second letter
of the name

Each author is subarranged by Table P-PZ40, unless
otherwise specified

0.13	C	

The author number is determined by the second letter
of the name

Each author is subarranged by Table P-PZ40, unless
otherwise specified

0.14	D	

The author number is determined by the second letter
of the name

Each author is subarranged by Table P-PZ40, unless
otherwise specified

0.15	E	

The author number is determined by the second letter
of the name

Each author is subarranged by Table P-PZ40, unless
otherwise specified

0.16	F	

The author number is determined by the second letter
of the name

Each author is subarranged by Table P-PZ40, unless
otherwise specified

0.17	G	

The author number is determined by the second letter
of the name

Each author is subarranged by Table P-PZ40, unless
otherwise specified

0.18	H	

The author number is determined by the second letter
of the name

Each author is subarranged by Table P-PZ40, unless
otherwise specified

0.19	I	

The author number is determined by the second letter
of the name

Each author is subarranged by Table P-PZ40, unless
otherwise specified

0.2	J	

The author number is determined by the second letter
of the name

Each author is subarranged by Table P-PZ40, unless
otherwise specified

0.21   K
                        The author number is determined by the second letter
                           of the name
                        Each author is subarranged by Table P-PZ40, unless
                           otherwise specified
0.22   L
                        The author number is determined by the second letter
                           of the name
                        Each author is subarranged by Table P-PZ40, unless
                           otherwise specified
0.23   M
                        The author number is determined by the second letter
                           of the name
                        Each author is subarranged by Table P-PZ40, unless
                           otherwise specified
0.24   N
                        The author number is determined by the second letter
                           of the name
                        Each author is subarranged by Table P-PZ40, unless
                           otherwise specified
0.25   O
                        The author number is determined by the second letter
                           of the name
                        Each author is subarranged by Table P-PZ40, unless
                           otherwise specified
0.26   P
                        The author number is determined by the second letter
                           of the name
                        Each author is subarranged by Table P-PZ40, unless
                           otherwise specified
0.27   Q
                        The author number is determined by the second letter
                           of the name
                        Each author is subarranged by Table P-PZ40, unless
                           otherwise specified
0.28   R
                        The author number is determined by the second letter
                           of the name
                        Each author is subarranged by Table P-PZ40, unless
                           otherwise specified
0.29   S
                        The author number is determined by the second letter
                           of the name
                        Each author is subarranged by Table P-PZ40, unless
                           otherwise specified
0.3   T
                        The author number is determined by the second letter
                           of the name
                        Each author is subarranged by Table P-PZ40, unless
                           otherwise specified

0.31	U	
		The author number is determined by the second letter of the name
		Each author is subarranged by Table P-PZ40, unless otherwise specified
0.32	V	
		The author number is determined by the second letter of the name
		Each author is subarranged by Table P-PZ40, unless otherwise specified
0.33	W	
		The author number is determined by the second letter of the name
		Each author is subarranged by Table P-PZ40, unless otherwise specified
0.34	X	
		The author number is determined by the second letter of the name
		Each author is subarranged by Table P-PZ40, unless otherwise specified
0.35	Y	
		The author number is determined by the second letter of the name
		Each author is subarranged by Table P-PZ40, unless otherwise specified
0.36	Z	
		The author number is determined by the second letter of the name
		Each author is subarranged by Table P-PZ40, unless otherwise specified

	Polyglot. Translations into several languages
	Polyglot. Translations into several languages
1.A1	General
1.A3	Poetry
1.A5	Drama
1.A8	Prose. Prose fiction
	English
1.E1	General
1.E3	Poetry
1.E5	Drama
1.E8	Prose. Prose fiction
	French
1.F1	General
1.F3	Poetry
1.F5	Drama
1.F8	Prose. Prose fiction
	German
1.G1	General
1.G3	Poetry
1.G5	Drama
1.G8	Prose. Prose fiction
	Italian
1.I1	General
1.I3	Poetry
1.I5	Drama
1.I8	Prose. Prose fiction
	Russian
1.R1	General
1.R3	Poetry
1.R5	Drama
1.R8	Prose. Prose fiction
	Spanish
1.S1	General
1.S3	Poetry
1.S5	Drama
1.S8	Fiction. Prose fiction
2	Other languages, A-Z

	Collected works
	Original editions and reprints. By date
0.A00-A99	To 1500
0.B00-B99	1500-1599
0.C00-C99	1600-1699
0.D00-D99	1700-1799
0.E00-E99	1800-1899
0.F00-F99	1900-1999
1.A-Z	Editions with commentary, etc. By editor, A-Z
2	Selected works
	Subarrange by editor, if given, or date
3	Selections. Anthologies. Extracts
	Subarrange by editor, if given, or date
4.A-Z	Translations (Collected or selected). By language, A-Z
	Subarrange by translator, if given, or date
5-22	Separate works. By title
	Only the more important have a special number or numbers assigned to them; the lesser works are to have Cutter numbers
	For subdivisions where one number is assigned to a work subarrange according to Table P-PZ41. For works with Cutter numbers, use Table P-PZ43
23	Doubtful, spurious works (Collections only)
24	Imitations. Adaptations. Parodies (Collections only)
25	Relation to the drama and the stage. Dramatization
26	Translations (Comparative studies, etc.)
	Illustrations (Portfolios, etc. without text, illustrations with quotations)
	Class at N8215, or with the special artists in NC-NE as the case may be
	Class illustrated editions with other editions
	Class portraits, etc. of the author with his biography
	Biography, criticism, etc.
29	Periodicals. Societies. Serials
30	Dictionaries, indexes, etc.
	Class here general encyclopedic dictionaries only
	For concordances and dictionaries, see 45
30.5	Historical sources and documents of the biography or author
	For sources of literary works, see 36-37
	Autobiographical works
31.A2	Autobiography. By date
31.A3-A39	Journals. Memoirs. By title
31.A4	Letters (Collections). By date
31.A41-A49	Letters to and from particular individuals. By correspondent (alphabetically)
31.A5-Z	General works
32	Special periods of the author's life
	Including early life, education, love and marriage, relation to women, relation to men, later life
33	Relations to contemporaries. Times, etc.
34	Homes and haunts. Local associations. Landmarks

	Biography, criticism, etc. -- Continued
35	Anniversaries. Celebrations. Memorial addresses. Iconography. Monuments. Relics. Museums, exhibitions, etc.
	Authorship
	Including manuscripts, sources, etc.
	For textual criticism, see 43
36	General works
37	Chronology of works
	Criticism and interpretation
	History
37.3	General works
37.4.A-Z	By region or country, A-Z
38	General works
39	Characters
41	Technique, plots, scenes, time, etc.
42.A-Z	Treatment and knowledge of special subjects, A-Z
42.A34	Aesthetics
42.A4	Allegory
42.A43	Allusions
42.A54	America
42.A56	Animism
42.A6	Arab countries
42.A615	Archetype
42.A62	Architecture
42.A63	Arianism
42.A66	Art
42.A7	Asia
42.B5	Bible
	Blackmail, see 42.E95
42.B58	Body, Human
42.B6	Books
42.B65	Botany
	Business, see 42.C65
42.C36	Calvinism
42.C4	Censorship
	Child and parent, see 42.P34
42.C46	Children's literature
42.C5	Ciphers
42.C56	Cities and towns
42.C65	Commerce. Business
42.C67	Conversation
42.C7	Criticism (the author as critic)
42.D25	Dance
42.D35	Death
42.D4	Devil
42.D45	Devotional literature
42.D52	Didactic literature
42.D56	Disguise
42.D57	Divorce
42.D6	Dogs
42.D64	Doubles
42.D68	Dramatic monologues

	Criticism and
	interpretation
	Treatment and knowledge
	of special subjects, A-Z -- Continued
42.D7	Dramatic works
42.D74	Dreams
42.D78	Drinking
42.D82	Duality
42.E25	Economics
42.E5	Emotions
42.E54	England
42.E63	Epitaphs
42.E8	Ethics
42.E85	Europe
42.E9	Evil
42.E95	Extortion. Blackmail
42.F35	Fairy tales
42.F36	Family
42.F43	Fear
42.F45	Feminism
42.F53	Fictional works
42.F6	Folklore
42.G4	Geography
42.G42	Geology
42.G43	Germany
42.G6	God
42.G63	Great Britain
42.G65	Greece
42.G7	Grotesque
42.G85	Guilt
42.H3	Happiness
42.H34	Hate
42.H4	Heraldry
42.H47	Heroes. Heroines
42.H5	History
42.H55	Home
42.H56	Homosexuality
	Human body, see 42.B58
42.H62	Humor. Satire
42.H94	Hypocrisy
42.I53	Indians
42.I58	Invocation
42.I82	Italy
42.J48	Jews
42.L27	Landscape
42.L3	Law
42.L48	Liberty
42.L5	Literature
42.L58	London (England)
42.L6	Love
42.M25	Manners and customs
42.M3	Marriage
42.M37	Masques

	Criticism and
	interpretation
	Treatment and knowledge
	of special subjects, A-Z -- Continued
42.M43	Medicine
42.M45	Memory
42.M47	Mesmerism
42.M53	Middle Ages
42.M55	Military science
42.M57	Misanthropy
42.M65	Monism
42.M67	Mother and child
42.M73	Muses
42.M87	Music
42.M95	Mysticism
42.M96	Myth
42.N2	Nature
42.O25	Occult
42.O5	Optimism
42.O73	Orient
42.O76	Orphans
42.P3	Paradise
42.P34	Parent and child
42.P36	Pastoral literature
42.P38	Patriarchy
42.P45	Performing arts
42.P5	Philosophy
42.P63	Poetic works
42.P64	Politics
42.P7	Prose
42.P74	Psychology
42.P76	Punishment
42.P8	Puritans
42.R27	Radicalism
42.R36	Readers
42.R37	Realism
42.R4	Religion
42.R63	Romanticism
42.R65	Rome
	Satire, see 42.H62
42.S3	Science
42.S34	Scotland
42.S36	Secrecy
42.S38	Self
42.S4	Semitic philology
42.S43	Senses and sensation
42.S44	Sentimentalism
42.S46	Settings
42.S47	Sex
42.S52	Shamanism
42.S55	Skepticism
42.S56	Slavery
42.S58	Social problems. Society

	Criticism and
	interpretation
	Treatment and knowledge
	of special subjects, A-Z -- Continued
42.S6	Socialism
	Society, see 42.S58
42.S68	Soviet Union
42.S72	Stage history
42.S88	Subconsciousness
42.S9	Subjectivity
42.S93	Suffering
42.S95	Sympathy
42.T5	Time
	Towns and cities, see 42.C56
42.T73	Travel
42.V56	Violence
42.W3	War
42.W48	West (U.S.)
42.W6	Women
42.W75	Writing
43	Textual criticism, commentaries, etc.
	Language, style, etc.
44	General works
45	Dictionaries. Concordances
46	Grammar
47	Versification, meter, rhythm, etc.
48	Dialect, etc.

	Collected works
	By date
0.A00-A99	To 1500
0.B00-B99	1500-1599
0.C00-C99	1600-1699
0.D00-D99	1700-1799
0.E00-E99	1800-1899
0.F00-F99	1900-1999
1	By editor, if given
2	Selected works. Selections
	Subarrange by editor, if given, or date
	Translations (Collected or selected)
3	Modern versions of early authors in the same language. By translator, if given, or date
4.A-Z	Other. By language, A-Z
	Subarrange by translator, if given, or date
5-10	Separate works. By title
	Subarrange each title by Table P-PZ41 or P-PZ43
11	Apocryphal, spurious works, etc. (Collections only)
	Illustrations
	Class at N8215, or with the special artists in NC-NE as the case may be
	Class illustrated editions with other editions
	Class portraits, etc., of the author with his biography
	Biography, criticism, etc.
12.A1-A5	Periodicals. Societies. Serials
12.A6-Z	Dictionaries, indexes, etc.
13.A3-A39	Autobiography, journals, memoirs. By title
13.A4	Letters (Collections). By date
13.A41-A49	Letters to and from particular individuals. By correspondent (alphabetically)
13.A5-Z	General works
	Criticism
14	General works
15	Textual. Manuscripts, etc.
	Special
16	Sources
17.A-Z	Other, A-Z
17.A33	Adolescence
17.A35	Aesthetics
17.A36	Aggressiveness
17.A6	Allegory
17.A62	Allusions
17.A63	Ambiguity
17.A64	Apocalyptic literature
17.A72	Architecture
17.A75	Art
17.A89	Authority
17.A9	Authorship
17.B52	Bible
17.B54	Biography (as a literary form)
17.B55	Biology

	Criticism
	Special
	Other, A-Z -- Continued
17.B57	Body, Human
17.B58	Book arts and sciences
17.B6	Books and reading
17.B8	Burlesque (Literature)
17.C47	Characters and characteristics
17.C5	China
17.C52	Cities and towns. City and town life
17.C53	Clergy
17.C56	Comic, The
17.C57	Commerce
17.C6	Courtesy
17.C7	Creation
17.C74	Cricket
17.C76	Crime
17.C8	Cuchulain
17.C84	Culture shock
17.D4	Death
17.D53	Didactic literature
17.D68	Dramatic production
17.D7	Dramatic works
17.D73	Dreams
17.D83	Dualism
17.E25	Economics
17.E3	Education
17.E46	England
17.E8	Ethics
17.E87	Europe
17.E9	Evil
17.F33	Fairies
17.F35	Family
17.F37	Fantasy
17.F44	Feminism
17.F5	Fictional works
17.F55	Film adaptations
17.F64	Folklore
17.F66	Food habits
17.F7	French literature. France
17.F74	Friendship
17.F87	Future
17.G42	Genealogy
17.G44	Geography
17.G47	Germany
17.G73	Greece
17.H34	Hate
17.H4	Heroes. Heroines
17.H5	History
17.H64	Hope
	Human body, see 17.B57
	Humor, see 17.S2
17.I33	Idealism

	Criticism
	Special
	Other, A-Z -- Continued
17.I35	Identity (Psychology)
17.I4	Imagination
17.I44	Immortality
17.I45	Imperialism
17.I46	Impressionism
17.I48	India
17.I5	Individualism
17.I52	Influence
17.I67	Ireland
17.I7	Irony
17.I8	Italy
17.J48	Jews
17.K56	Kinship
17.L3	Landscape
17.L35	Laudatory poetry
17.L36	Law
17.L48	Letters (in literature)
17.L5	Literature
17.L65	Love
17.L88	Luxury
17.M3	Marriage
17.M34	Marvelous, The
17.M36	Masculinity (Psychology)
17.M4	Medicine
17.M42	Medievalism. Middle Ages
17.M45	Mental illness
17.M47	Metamorphosis
	Middle Ages, see 17.M42
17.M55	Mimesis
17.M6	Money
17.M64	Mothers
17.M74	Music
17.M8	Mysticism
17.M82	Myth
17.M83	Mythology
17.N3	Nature
17.O25	Occultism
17.O74	Orient
17.P3	Parody
17.P34	Pastoral literature
17.P4	Performing arts
17.P44	Pessimism
17.P5	Philosophy
17.P54	Plots
17.P58	Poetic works
17.P6	Political and social views
17.P63	Power (Social sciences)
17.P67	Prose
17.P68	Proverbs
17.P7	Prudence

	Criticism
	Special
	Other, A-Z -- Continued
17.P8	Psychology
17.P87	Puritanism
17.Q5	Quests
17.Q53	Quietude
17.R3	Race problems
	Reading, see 17.B6
17.R37	Realism
17.R4	Religion
17.R47	Revenge
17.R5	Rivers
17.R6	Rogues and vagabonds
17.R64	Romanticism
17.S2	Satire. Humor
17.S3	Scatology
17.S35	Science
17.S42	Secrecy
17.S44	Self
17.S46	Settings
17.S48	Sex
17.S54	Silence
	Social views, see 17.P6
17.S6	Socialism
17.S7	Soldiers
17.S75	Stage history
17.S78	Study and teaching
17.S92	Sublime, The
17.S93	Suicide
17.S95	Symbolism
17.S97	Sympathy
17.T4	Technique
17.T53	Thought and thinking
17.T54	Time
17.T7	Tragic, The
17.T72	Tragicomedy
17.T73	Translations
17.T74	Travel
17.U76	Utopias
17.V4	Versification
17.V56	Visions
17.W37	War
17.W43	Weather
17.W6	Women
18	Language. Grammar. Style

	Collected works
	By date
0.A00-A99	To 1500
0.B00-B99	1500-1599
0.C00-C99	1600-1699
0.D00-D99	1700-1799
0.E00-E99	1800-1899
0.F00-F99	1900-1999
1	By editor, if given
2	Selected works. Selections
	Subarrange by editor, if given, or date
	Translations (Collected or selected)
3.A2A-Z	Modern versions of early authors in the same language. By translator, if given, or date
3.A3-Z	Other. By language, A-Z
	Subarrange by translator, if given, or date
4.A-Z	Separate works. By title
	Subarrange each title by Table P-PZ43
5	Apocryphal, spurious works, etc., (Collections only)
	Illustrations
	Class at N8215, or with the special artists in NC-NE as the case may be
	Class illustrated editions with other editions
	Class portraits, etc., of the author with his biography
	Biography, criticism, etc.
6.A1-A19	Periodicals. Societies. Serials
6.A2-A3	Dictionaries, indexes, etc.
6.A31-A39	Autobiography, journals, memoirs. By title
6.A4	Letters (Collections). By date
6.A41-A49	Letters to and from particular individuals. By correspondent (alphabetically)
6.A5-Z	General works
	Criticism
7	General works
8.A-Z	Special, A-Z
8.A33	Adolescence
8.A35	Aesthetics
8.A36	Aggressiveness
8.A6	Allegory
8.A62	Allusions
8.A63	Ambiguity
8.A64	Apocalyptic literature
8.A72	Architecture
8.A75	Art
8.A89	Authority
8.A9	Authorship
8.B52	Bible
8.B54	Biography (as a literary form)
8.B55	Biology
8.B57	Body, Human
8.B58	Book arts and sciences
8.B6	Books and reading

Criticism
   Special, A-Z -- Continued

8.B8	Burlesque (Literature)
8.C47	Characters and characteristics
8.C5	China
8.C52	Cities and towns. City and town life
8.C53	Clergy
8.C56	Comic, The
8.C57	Commerce
8.C6	Courtesy
8.C7	Creation
8.C74	Cricket
8.C76	Crime
8.C8	Cuchulain
8.C84	Culture shock
8.D4	Death
8.D53	Didactic literature
8.D68	Dramatic production
8.D7	Dramatic works
8.D73	Dreams
8.D83	Dualism
8.E25	Economics
8.E3	Education
8.E46	England
8.E8	Ethics
8.E87	Europe
8.E9	Evil
8.F33	Fairies
8.F35	Family
8.F37	Fantasy
8.F44	Feminism
8.F5	Fictional works
8.F55	Film adaptations
8.F64	Folklore
8.F66	Food habits
8.F7	French literature. France
8.F74	Friendship
8.F87	Future
8.G42	Genealogy
8.G44	Geography
8.G47	Germany
8.G73	Greece
8.H34	Hate
8.H4	Heroes. Heroines
8.H5	History
8.H64	Hope
	Human body, see 8.B57
	Humor, see 8.S2
8.I33	Idealism
8.I35	Identity (Psychology)
8.I4	Imagination
8.I44	Immortality
8.I45	Imperialism

	Criticism
	Special, A-Z -- Continued
8.I46	Impressionism
8.I48	India
8.I5	Individualism
8.I52	Influence
8.I67	Ireland
8.I7	Irony
8.I8	Italy
8.J48	Jews
8.K56	Kinship
8.L3	Landscape
8.L33	Language
8.L35	Laudatory poetry
8.L36	Law
8.L48	Letters (in literature)
8.L5	Literature
8.L65	Love
8.L88	Luxury
8.M3	Marriage
8.M34	Marvelous, The
8.M36	Masculinity (Psychology)
8.M4	Medicine
8.M42	Medievalism. Middle Ages
8.M45	Mental illness
8.M47	Metamorphosis
	Middle Ages, see 8.M42
8.M55	Mimesis
8.M6	Money
8.M74	Music
8.M8	Mysticism
8.M82	Myth
8.M83	Mythology
8.N3	Nature
8.O25	Occultism
8.O74	Orient
8.P3	Parody
8.P34	Pastoral literature
8.P4	Performing arts
8.P44	Pessimism
8.P5	Philosophy
8.P54	Plots
8.P58	Poetic works
8.P6	Political and social views
8.P63	Power (Social sciences)
8.P67	Prose
8.P68	Proverbs
8.P7	Prudence
8.P8	Psychology
8.P87	Puritanism
8.Q5	Quests
8.Q53	Quietude
8.R3	Race problems

	Criticism
	Special, A-Z -- Continued
	Reading, see 8.B6
8.R37	Realism
8.R4	Religion
8.R47	Revenge
8.R5	Rivers
8.R6	Rogues and vagabonds
8.R64	Romanticism
8.S2	Satire. Humor
8.S3	Scatology
8.S35	Science
8.S42	Secrecy
8.S44	Self
8.S46	Settings
8.S48	Sex
8.S54	Silence
	Social views, see 8.P6
8.S6	Socialism
8.S7	Soldiers
8.S75	Stage history
8.S78	Study and teaching
8.S8	Style
8.S92	Sublime, The
8.S93	Suicide
8.S95	Symbolism
8.S97	Sympathy
8.T4	Technique
8.T53	Thought and thinking
8.T54	Time
8.T7	Tragic, The
8.T72	Tragicomedy
8.T73	Translations
8.T74	Travel
8.U76	Utopias
8.V4	Versification
8.V56	Visions
8.W37	War
8.W43	Weather
8.W6	Women

0	Texts. By editor, if given, or date
	Including texts with commentaries
1	Selections. By editor, if given, or date
	Translations
2	Modern versions of early works in the same language.
	By translator, if given, or date
3.A-Z	Other. By language, A-Z
	Subarrange by translator, if given, or date
4	Criticism

	Collected works
0.A1	To 1800. By date
	1800-
0.A2	By date
0.A5A-Z	By editor, if given
0.A6-Z	Translations (Collected or selected). By language, A-Z
	Subarrange by translator, if given, or date
1	Selected works. Selections. By editor, if given, or date
2.A-Z	Separate works. By title, A-Z
	Subarrange each title by Table P-PZ43
	Biography, criticism, etc.
3.A1-A29	Periodicals. Societies. Serials
3.A3	Dictionaries, indexes, etc. By date
3.A4-A43	Autobiography, journals, memoirs. By title
3.A44	Letters (Collections). By date
3.A45-A49	Letters to and from particular individuals. By correspondent (alphabetically)
3.A5-Z	General works
4	Criticism
	Where only four numbers are provided, class Criticism with Biography

	Collected works
1.A1	By date
1.A2	By editor, if given
1.A3A-Z	Translations (Collected or selected). By language, A-Z
1.A4	Selected works. Selections. By date
1.A5-Z	Separate works. By title
	Biography and criticism
2.A2	Dictionaries, indexes, etc. By date
2.A3-A39	Autobiography, journals, memoirs. By title
2.A4	Letters (Collections). By date
2.A41-A49	Letters to and from particular individuals. By correspondent (alphabetically)
2.A5-Z	General works

	Collected works
0.A1	By date
0.A11-A19	By editor, if given
	Translations (Collected or selected)
	Where the original language is English, French or German, omit numbers for original language
0.A2-A29	English. By translator, if given, or date
0.A3-A39	French. By translator, if given, or date
0.A4-A49	German. By translator, if given, or date
0.A5-A59	Other. By language
0.A6	Selected works. Selections. By date
0.A61-A78	Separate works. By title
	Biography and criticism
0.A79	Dictionaries, indexes, etc. By date
0.A8-A829	Autobiography, journals, memoirs. By title
0.A83	Letters (Collections). By date
0.A84-A849	Letters to and from particular individuals. By correspondent (alphabetically)
0.A85-Z	General works

	Collected works
.x	By date
.xA11-.xA19	By editor, if given
	Translations (Collected or selected)
	Where the original language is English, French, or German, omit numbers for original language
.xA2-.xA29	English. By translator, if given, or date
.xA3-.xA39	French. By translator, if given, or date
.xA4-.xA49	German. By translator, if given, or date
.xA5-.xA59	Other. By language
.xA6	Selected works. Selections. By date
.xA61-.xA78	Separate works. By title
	Biography and criticism
.xA79	Dictionaries, indexes, etc. By date
.xA8-.xA829	Autobiography, journals, memoirs. By title
.xA83	Letters (Collections). By date
.xA84-.xA849	Letters to and from particular individuals. By correspondent (alphabetically)
.xA85-.xZ	General works

	Collected works
0.A1	By date
0.A11-A13	By editor, if given
0.A14	Collected prose works. By date
0.A15	Collected fiction. By date
0.A16	Collected essays. By date
0.A17	Collected poems. By date
0.A19	Collected plays. By date
	Translations (Collected or selected)
	Where the original language is English, French or German, omit numbers for original language in P-PZ39 0.A2-0.A49
0.A199	Modern versions of early authors in the same language. By date
0.A1995	Polyglot. By date
0.A2-A29	English. By translator, if given, or date
0.A3-A39	French. By translator, if given, or date
0.A4-A49	German. By translator, if given, or date
0.A5-A59	Other. By language
0.A6	Selected works. Selections. By date
0.A61-Z48	Separate works. By title
	Subarrange each work by Table P-PZ43
	Biography and criticism
0.Z481-Z489	Periodicals. Societies. Serials
0.Z49	Dictionaries, indexes, etc. By date
0.Z5A3-Z5A39	Autobiography, journals, memoirs. By title
0.Z5A4	Letters (Collections). By date
0.Z5A41-Z5A49	Letters to and from particular individuals. By correspondent (Alphabetically)
0.Z5A5-Z5Z	General works

	Collected works
.x	By date
.xA11-.xA13	By editor, if given
.xA14	Collected prose works. By date
.xA15	Collected fiction. By date
.xA16	Collected essays. By date
.xA17	Collected poems. By date
.xA19	Collected plays. By date
	Translations (Collected or selected)
	Where the original language is English, French or
	German, omit numbers for original language in P-PZ40
	.xA2-.xA49
.xA199	Modern versions of early authors in the same language.
	By date
.xA1995	Polyglot. By date
.xA2-.xA29	English. By translator, if given, or date
.xA3-.xA39	French. By translator, if given, or date
.xA4-.xA49	German. By translator, if given, or date
.xA5-.xA59	Other. By language
.xA6	Selected works. Selections. By date
.xA61-.Z458	Separate works. By title
	Biography and criticism
.xZ4581-.xZ4589	Periodicals. Societies. Serials
.xZ459	Dictionaries, indexes, etc. By date
.xZ46-.xZ479	Autobiography, journals, memoirs. By title
.xZ48	Letters (Collections). By date
.xZ481-.xZ499	Letters to and from particular individuals. By
	correspondent (alphabetically)
.xZ5-.xZ999	General works

	Texts
0.A1	By date
0.A2A-Z	By editor, if given, A-Z
0.A21-A29	Modern versions of early works in the same language. By translator, if given, or date
0.A3	Selections. By date
	Translations
	Where the original language is English, French or German, omit numbers for original language
0.A31-A39	English. By translator, if given, or date
0.A4-A49	French. By translator, if given, or date
0.A5-A59	German. By translator, if given, or date
0.A6-A69	Other. By language
0.A7-Z	Criticism

	In Table P-PZ42 .x, .x2, and .x3 represent successive Cutter numbers, as, for example: .P4, .P5, .P6
.x	Collected works. Selected works. By date
	For anonymous works or for authors with only one surviving work, the first number is used: .x date, Texts. By date; .xA-Z Texts. By editor, A-Z
.xA-Z	Separate works. By title, A-Z
	For anonymous works or for authors with only one surviving work, the first number is used: .x date, Texts. By date; .xA-Z Texts. By editor, A-Z
.x2A-Z	Translations. By language, A-Z
	Further subarranged by date
.x3A-Z	Criticism

	In Table P-PZ43, .x, .x2, and .x3 represent successive Cutter numbers, as, for example: .F6, .F7, .F8 or .F66, .F67, .F68
	In the case of works where division .x2 is inapplicable the numbers may be modified by using two Cutter numbers only, as .F4, .F5 or .F4, .F41
.x	Texts. By date
.xA-Z	Translations. By language
.xA3-.xA39	Modern versions of early works in same language. By translator, if given, or date
.xA399	Polyglot
.xA4-.xZ	Other languages, A-Z
.x2	Selections. By date
.x3	Criticism

	Table for authors (2 successive Cutter nos.)
.x	By date
.xA11-.xA13	By editor, if given
.xA15	Collected fiction. By date
.xA16	Collected essays. By date
.xA17	Collected poems. By date
.xA19	Collected plays. By date
	Translations (Collected or selected)
	Where the original language is English, French or German, omit numbers for original language
.xA2-.xA29	English. By translator, if given, or date
.xA3-.xA39	French. By translator, if given, or date
.xA4-.xA49	German. By translator, if given, or date
.xA5-.xA59	Other. By language
.xA6	Selections. By date
.xA61-.xZ95	Separate works. By title
.xZ96	Spurious works. Adaptations. Parodies (Collections only)
	Biography and criticism
.x2A1-.x2A19	Periodicals. Societies. Serials
.x2A2	Dictionaries, indexes, etc. By date
.x2A31-.x2A39	Autobiography, journals, memoirs. By title
.x2A4	Letters (Collections.) By date
.x2A41-.x2A49	Letters to and from particular individuals. By correspondent (alphabetically)
.x2A5-.x2Z	General works

	Even though actual instructions are not made in the P classification schedules to apply this table, it is to be used under individual biography numbers for literary critics and historians, actors, journalists, teachers, philologists, and other persons not covered by provisions for literary authors
	.x = Cutter number for the person
.xA2	Collected works. By date
.xA25	Selected works. Selections. By date
	Including quotations
.xA3	Autobiography, diaries, etc. By date
.xA4	Letters. By date
.xA5	Speeches, essays, and lectures. By date
.xA6-.xZ	Biography and criticism